CATCHING GOD'S HEART

BOOKS COMPILED BY FRANK DeCENSO, JR.

Amazed by the Power of God
God's Supernatural Power in You

ALSO AVAILABLE FROM DESTINY IMAGE PUBLISHERS
BOOKS BY MARK A. DUPONT
BOOKS BY DAVID RAVENHILL

CATCHING GOD'S HEART

The Wisdom and Power of Intimacy

Compiled by Frank DeCenso Jr.

DESTINY IMAGE® PUBLISHERS, INC.
P.O. Box 310, Shippensburg, PA 17257-0310
"Speaking to the Purposes of God for This Generation and for the Generations to Come."

This book and all other Destiny Image, Revival Press, MercyPlace, Fresh Bread, Destiny Image Fiction, and Treasure House books are available at Christian bookstores and distributors worldwide.

For a U.S. bookstore nearest you, call 1-800-722-6774.
For more information on foreign distributors, call 717-532-3040.
Reach us on the Internet: www.destinyimage.com.

Trade Paper ISBN 13: 978-0-7684-3250-3
Hardcover ISBN 978-0-7684-3440-8
Large Print ISBN 978-0-7684-3441-5
Ebook ISBN 978-0-7684-9119-7

For Worldwide Distribution, Printed in the U.S.A.
1 2 3 4 5 6 7 8 9 10 11 / 13 12 11 10

Contents

Introduction

"I must decline your invitation owing to a subsequent engagement."

—Oscar Wilde, Irish dramatist,
novelist, and poet (1854–1900)

The purpose of this compilation is to instruct and encourage believers about intimacy with God and the unfathomable riches that accompany a lifestyle of such intimacy.

As a result of Jesus' death on the Cross, the Word of God contains many invitations for us to engage in close, intimate fellowship with Him. However, invitations can be intrusive. Think about it.

Someone invites you to dinner or a movie or a ballgame, and then it's up to you to either accept or decline. The burden is thrust upon you. You must make the decision whether to accept the invitation given to you or decline it. How will your response make the other person feel?

Did they only ask you out of a feeling of obligation because you had invited them to something in the past? Is their invitation sincere, or are you being asked because you happen to be around another person or persons who are being asked at that time—perhaps leading to a "pity invite" ("I'd better invite so-and-so or they'll feel bad.")?

Invitations can also be edifying. Maybe the pastor of your church invites you to lunch for a chat. Maybe an old friend invites you over for a game of Scrabble on a night when you had absolutely no plans whatsoever and were thinking, "Well, looks like another lonely weekend at home."

There are also invitations that come from unexpectedly pleasant sources and literally cause us to drop any and all plans we may have had so we can accept the invite that is too good to decline. The president of your company invites you and your family over for a pool party on the day you planned on going golfing; perhaps someone invites you to go to the World Series with them during the week you were going to weed the garden.

Plans can be dropped if we want to engage in something else we've been invited to participate in. How do we determine which invites to accept or decline? Usually we evaluate the invite, the timing, our circumstances, the inviter, and maybe some other things.

However, there is one invitation that transcends all other possible invitations and should never cause us to critically evaluate it. The response to this invite should always be a passionate, "Yes!"

Listen! I am standing at the door and knocking! If anyone hears My voice and opens the door I will come into his home and share a meal with him, and he with Me (Revelation 3:20 NET).

The issuer of this invite is Jesus Christ, the King of Glory, the One who purchased our eternal salvation with His sinless blood.

This invitation is not a one-time invite like a friend's invitation to a ball game or a chess tournament. Jesus invites us to a continuing communion with Him. This invite never expires, and we are the only ones who could decline the offer. Without getting too technical with this verse, I simply want to point out a few things that hopefully will encourage us to embrace and accept this wonderful invitation from Jesus.

Notice first of all that Jesus is "standing"—waiting for us to open the door. Our lack of response to His arrival at our residence doesn't deter Him from continuing His request for us to let Him in. He is pursuing us vigorously, unrelentingly, and lovingly. He desperately wants to spend time with us in intimate communion, and He will always try to pull us away from the worthless things of this world to spend precious time with Him. He loves us more than our picture of a deity sitting on a throne somewhere saying mechanically, "I love you." Rather, He loves us with a love that pursues us to spend time with him. This becomes a little clearer as we examine the "knocking."

When Jesus says He is "knocking," He isn't lightly tapping on the screen door, hoping to cause our dog to bark, alerting us to a visitor. The word "knocking" used here is the Greek word *krouo*, and it means, "to knock with the knuckles with a loud rap, with a heavy blow." Jesus is determined to let us know He is at our home and wants to come in to be with us. It's as if the King of Glory is saying, "I'm here! I'm here! Please open your door! I want to spend some time with you."

Let's be realistic for a moment. The majority of people on planet earth have lives that include some form of work, family time, and leisure. Yet Jesus is constantly knocking to bring us to a decision of letting Him in. He doesn't want to be left out of any part of our lives. Are our jobs more important than making some time to spend in solitude with Him? Can't we spend time with Him while working or washing the clothes or weeding the garden? Of course we can. Jesus engaged in both continual communion and situational solitude with His Father, all during a life that included spending countless hours ministering to people and teaching His disciples. He is our model for life. If He did it, so can we.

Jesus wouldn't knock to gain entrance to our homes if He knew His presence would disturb our lives. His presence enhances our lives, blesses our lives, and gives meaning to our activities. He loves us and wants to "hang out" with us 24/7. The only question is—do we want to spend that kind of time with Him? Do we desire to accept His invitation to "share a meal with us"?

If we determine to spend intimate, quality time with Jesus but don't know how, we should ask Him: "Lord, show me how to spend time with You continually and in solitude, even in the midst of my busy and hectic life." I can offer a few suggestions.

1. Make *each and every moment* an opportunity to be with Jesus. Wherever you are, invite Him to join you in fellowship while you live your life.

2. Make *a time* to simply "hang out" with Jesus. Find a quiet room, a comfortable chair, a secluded bench in the

park—wherever you can be uninterrupted in quiet time with Him.

During these moments and times, try not to intercede or pray for anything specific or talk too much. Just ask Him to come and be with you—accepting His invite to "dine" with Him.

If we have not heard His knocking, perhaps the things of this world have drowned Him out. Listen. Listen closely. Can you hear Him? He wants to be with you. He's knocking and calling out your name. He wants to share intimate fellowship with you and accompany you on life's trails and trials.

Knock. Knock. He's there. Will you open the door?

Frank DeCenso Jr.

CHAPTER 1

A Great Mystery

DR. CHE AHN

This is a great mystery, but I speak concerning Christ and the Church (Ephesians 5:32 NKJV).

Such a great mystery! There are a myriad of choices God could have made to describe the relationship of Jesus and His people. Yet there is nothing comparable to being called His Bride and called unto a union of marriage with the Lord. This is the most intimate of all relationships. There is such a tenderness and affection in this choice—such an exclusivity and passion. The analogy is such a telling comparison about the nature and intimacy of God the Father and Jesus the Lord *with us.*

It's full of wonder and awe. While much of this book is given to describing the personal intimacy into which we have each been invited with the Lord, I chose to address a different paradigm. It's the paradigm of us, as His corporate Body, being called into corporate intimacy with our Bridegroom, Jesus.

There is nothing unholy or perverse in such an analogy. The written Word of God did not establish this archetype to in any way suggest a sexual union or a licentious connotation, as the world might place on such a parallel. Rather, I believe this mystery was given to allow those hungry seekers of a relational God to come into a divine understanding of the rights and privileges of this sacred spiritual union in eternity and the wonder of its earthly prototype now. Having this understanding can change the way we live, the way we view human relationships, and the way we honor and develop our spiritual identity with the Godhead.

A GARDEN BEGINNING

Why are we called to intimacy with the Lord Himself? It seems clear that we were designed to be His helpmate—the fulfillment and object of God's love. This is the same intent as husband and wife in a marriage. Beginning in Genesis, God sought out a personal relationship with us. He would walk and talk in the cool of the evening in the garden with Adam. Yet it wasn't enough. God "created one comparable"—a wife for Adam to help him better understand intimacy with another and with Him. The awesome privilege of intimacy unfolds throughout the Bible, consummating in the marriage supper of the Lamb with us as His bride.

The Body of Christ is clearly gaining a revelation of this intimacy with Jesus on a personal level, as is evidenced in the form and content of our worship and the change in our services and personal quiet times.

Our highest individual pursuit is to *"know Christ"* (see Phil. 3:10). Yet this intimacy takes on a whole new dimension as we consider Jesus' ultimate quest: To have us corporately for His Bride! A blueprint is found in Ephesians 5.

Since the Word describes this analogy as a "mystery," I claim no conclusive revelation about it. I simply hope to share insight into the mystery as it has made me love the Lord, my spouse, and myself more in response to His heart call to intimacy.

THE BLUEPRINT OF A BRIDE

Wives, submit to your own husbands, as to the Lord. For the husband is head of the wife, as also Christ is head of the church; and He is the Savior of the body. Therefore, just as the church is subject to Christ, so let the wives be to their own husbands in everything. Husbands, love your wives, just as Christ also loved the church and gave Himself for her, that He might sanctify and cleanse her with the washing of water by the word, that He might present her to Himself a glorious church, not having spot or wrinkle or any such thing, but that she should be holy and without blemish. So husbands ought to love their own wives as their own bodies; he who loves his wife loves himself. For no one ever hated his own flesh, but nourishes and cherishes it, just as the Lord does the church. For we are members of His body, of His flesh and of His bones. "For this reason a man shall leave his father and mother and be

joined to his wife, and the two shall become one flesh." This is
a great mystery, but I speak concerning Christ and the church.
Nevertheless let each one of you in particular so love his own
wife as himself, and let the wife see that she respects her hus-
band (Ephesians 5:22-33 NKJV).

This mystery of the marriage of a man and a woman and their conse-
quent oneness is an exciting parallel of Christ and the church. It is clearly
intentional and honorable. It is not static, such as a "redeemed people"
(though we are), or a mere classification, such as a "remnant" (though
this is also true). A bride is one that is sought out and won, valued, fought
for, and defended. For better or for worse, she is a chosen mate for life!
Imagine the love Jesus has for us to choose us as His Bride!

Surely Christ could have chosen us as *servants*. We know He
is gladdened by obedience and humility. He requires it from any
true disciple. Servants were expected to fulfill their obligations and
expect nothing more in return. Some went beyond what was due.
They were honored and considered members of the family. Many
chose to stay with their masters even when they were free to go.
Such servants defined themselves by their relationship with their
masters through the piercing of their ears with an awl (see Exod.
21:5-7; Deut. 15:16-18 NKJV).

A bride is one that is sought out and won, valued,
fought for, and defended. For better or for worse,
she is a chosen mate for life!

Such a depth of commitment suggests a depth of relationship,
respect, and homage. Yet servanthood is quite limited when compared

to other kinds of relationships found in the Bible. Sadly, many who profess Christ never enjoy anything more than being a servant. They do not understand God's invitation to "more." Certainly, we are His servants forever, but this is not the sole purpose or limitation of our relationship.

God could have chosen *friendship* for His model of Christ and the Church. Early on in Scripture, we find God speaking face to face with Moses *"as a man speaks to His friend"* (Exod. 33:11 NKJV). Moses was a man of rare privilege in his relationship with the Lord. His friendship was transforming, as we see when he returned from the mountain after meeting with God. His face was ablaze with God's presence.

"A friend loves at all times" (Prov. 17:17). Surely, that is a description of God's love for us. In a friendship, you find valued loyalty through good times and bad. Friends have trust for each other, gratitude, and enjoyment. Friends even have a special place in their hearts for each other and will defend one another when necessary. You can plainly see this special agape love in David and Jonathan's friendship as recounted in First Samuel. Verse 18 says their souls *"were knit."* I believe this means their hearts were voluntarily interwoven to a high degree.

We are friends with God. Many believers rightly aspire to friendship, for it far outweighs a mere servant bond. Unfortunately, they go no further. Yet friendship with the Lord could never be the closest bond.

How about an analogy of a *treasured child?* We are children of God, just as the Scripture states (see Rom. 8:16). A child is blood-born of the parents—a kinship unlike any other. A child receives a special place of honor and has access to all which belongs to the parents. There is caring, kindness, and love far different from that for a friend or an outsider. There is resemblance to the birth parents, just as we resemble God and are made in His image. There is great protection and provision and even inheritance afforded to a child, just as we receive from the Lord.

Yet a child is limited in understanding and maturity and even capacity for intimacy. God was looking for a *mate*. He wanted one called *beside* Him as a worthy, comparable, and intimate partner. When God chose to call His Church His Bride, He declared His intention for us to have the awesome honor of an exclusive relationship of the highest order. He desires for us to have an unbreakable covenant bond and enjoy the depths of love and security that cannot be found elsewhere. This best describes marriage alone.

INTIMACY DEFINED

For this chapter, I define intimacy as the highest and most vulnerable, personal, and private form of sharing and bonding between individuals. The greatest intimacy given to us by the Lord in this life is that of a man and a woman in marriage. Only here can a *supernatural* union be formed where the two *"become one"* in body, soul, *and spirit* (see Matt. 19:5-6). *This, too, is a mystery. I believe it only takes place by the power of the Holy Spirit in the consummation of the marriage of a man and wife and continues to grow in time with the relationship.*

While we may have "intimate" friends or family, the meaning usually connotes special people who have more history with us, more shared activities and memories, and more access to our lives. It also conveys a very high trust. While the world tries to pervert this concept by extending it to "same-sex" relationships or extramarital sex, it is not the same as the masterful creation of intimacy God intended.

The other great intimacy of our life is that which we have privately and exclusively with the Lord Himself. It is an unparalleled privilege:

> *Only one thing I have desired of the Lord, that will I seek: that*
> *I may dwell in the house of the Lord all the days of my life,*
> *to behold the beauty of the Lord, and to inquire in His temple*
> (Psalms 27:4 NKJV).

I know of no greater joy than the hours I spend beholding the Lord in His beauty and His majesty as I meditate upon Him. There is incomparable joy as I am filled with wonder, awe, and gratitude as I gaze intently on His face. I love to hear His voice, His direction, His heart. I love to know He cares about my heart and that He shares my dreams and listens to me. It is not a one-way relationship, but a deep oneness.

This intimacy births transformation in me. I am able to walk in a confidence and love that transcends anything gained by natural logic, positive thinking, worldly love, or the insights of a motivational speaker. This intimacy changes everything about my life and my interaction with others. Christ, not I, becomes my total and perfect source of life.

I say with sorrow that many people do not want this type of relationship. I believe if they had ever understood or enjoyed it for a moment, they could not resist. Many may serve God out of a heartfelt obedience, yet never share the joy of being His partner as a husband or a wife can be to each other.

I want to be His spouse. I want all that comes with that great privilege. I know of nothing else that fuels me with greater desire to serve Him and see His Kingdom established than personal intimacy with the Lord of lords and the King of kings. Nothing compels me with purer motives, greater endurance, or a more accurate representation of Christ on this earth than the fruit of walking in the intimacy of His love and total acceptance.

Yet there is coming a day when we will transcend even the incomparable greatness *of individual intimacy* with the Lord as we come together *as His Bride.*

An untold experience of *exponential oneness* awaits us!

WOOING US

Our glorious Bridegroom is wooing us now. This is an element not found in many relationships. There is romance, pursuit, and cherishing that endears us to Him, and Him to us. I believe this occurs when we worship.

Nothing compels me with purer motives, greater endurance, or a more accurate representation of Christ on this earth than the fruit of walking in the intimacy of His love and total acceptance.

Worship opens our hearts and reveals our hidden secrets and needs. We are aware of our vulnerability. Because the Lord is a safe and trustworthy love, we can allow our hearts to be further exposed each time we are in His presence. Many ministers and denominations do not or have not felt comfortable with what is called "intimate worship." Yet I believe it is a pure and holy expression of love through heartfelt adoration. We respond to the invitation of Jesus to come into the inner court as His beloved.

There are three places of worship found in the Old Testament temple model—the outer court, the inner court, and the Holy of Holies. In our personal relationship with Jesus, I believe we can choose how close we want to be to our Lord, or how far into the Holy Place we will go.

Just as in the models of relationship we examined—servant, friend, child, or spouse—we will often choose the level of intimacy or privilege with the Lord that we have been taught or feel comfortable with. Yet we need to fully realize that not only are we invited to His Wedding Supper, *we have been proposed to as His Bride!* Certainly this means we have access to the most intimate level of worship with Him.

No longer is this just to be found in a private setting, either. There is nothing obscene or exhibitionist about raising your arms in a display of love to Jesus or whispering personal words of adulation to Him. What is perhaps new to some is the unbridled corporate worship coming forth as we near the end of this age.

Certainly, the Lord is not ashamed of His bride or her exuberance! As on a wedding day, the Groom wants to show off the beauty of His beloved and have everyone gaze upon her. As we are yielding to Him as His Bride, He is taking us aside to the bridal chamber where He shares with us His deepest secrets and heals us where we are broken or untrusting. Our wholeness begins now.

COVENANT NOW

We know that God has already established a covenant with us as His people through His Son's sacrificial death on the Cross. The price God paid is incomprehensible, and the blessings and benefits of that covenant are simply too numerous to record. Surely salvation alone would be great enough. Yet we stand in an hour now where the King's desire is to reveal an even deeper covenant—one of intimacy with His chosen people.

This is affirmed by God's *mystery* of choosing the marriage analogy to describe the way of Christ and the Church. More than just intimacy, this analogy consummates in us becoming one with Christ supernaturally as do a husband and wife.

Why would God choose this highest and most demanding of all relationships to describe His union with us? One reason I believe is because it can be the most rewarding of all relationships. This is because of its exclusive, private nature and a shared vulnerability that is unparalleled.

While the union of a man and a woman may require the most attention and investment of all relationships, it is meant to continually flourish and provide mutual reward and return.

I see that as an ongoing picture of Christ's desire for relationship with us. Marriage should be the safest place on earth to get healed, delivered, and set free as you share yourself with that one person in irrevocable covenant. You become one in increasing measure through mutual experiences. You become freed of the chains of shame that have interwoven your life as you are unconditionally accepted by your mate. You have the opportunity to experience joys and sorrows unique to you alone, and to decide for yourselves the direction and goals of your union.

Your lives are voluntarily laid down one for another. You become a song sung together that is a melody no one else can play. It is intensely and ultimately the highest bond of oneness on earth.

Another major reason I believe God would choose us as His bride is because marriage is the only relationship called to bear children. Matthew 16:18 tells us that God will build His church. To do this, He is looking to reproduce Himself in the earth through His Bride.

Christ is not looking for a Church that wants to be His "girlfriend" or have an occasional "date." The difference of intimacy in dating and marriage is total. Many would prefer that lessened commitment. God, however, is serious about having a *Bride.* She is to be without spot or wrinkle, holy and without blemish (see Eph. 5:27 NKJV). *He will accomplish this if we will fully let go of our own control and allow Him to prepare us.*

MUTUAL INITIATIVE AND GROWING UP

The Bible says of our earthly marriages that the husband is to "wash" his wife with the Word (see Eph. 5:26-27 NKJV). This shows initiative and responsibility on the part of the groom to present the wife pure. If we are the Bride of Christ, that means He chooses to wash us and present us clean, too. Most of us know that holiness and righteousness are not something *we* can "achieve." In fact, the Word says our own righteousness is *"as filthy rags"* (Isa. 64:6 KJV). If we choose to flow with the Lord, it is certain we will be made clean. It comes not out of rote obedience but out of holy love. Jesus will wash us through His power and grace. Just as He first loved us and he paid the price for our salvation, He pays again for our privilege of being presented rightly as a bride before God.

Another interesting insight into this "washing" verse is the meaning of the "word" itself. It speaks of His cleansing us not with just a recital of the *logos* verses or text found in the Holy Bible. This particular derivation of "word" speaks of the *rhema* personal and current revelation spoken uniquely from His heart to ours. It is not a "one size fits all" word. Rather it is insight and love only an intimate partner could appropriately and constructively give to their mate. He knows how to speak over us in such a way to conform us to holiness. Jesus is jealous for each and every one of us and will share us with no one else. He defends us and protects us as would the most ardent lover.

Jesus is jealous for each and every one of us and will share us with no one else. He defends us and protects us as would the most ardent lover.

However, as His beloved, we have responsibility, too. We must no longer refuse the grace to grow up and be married. It's time to work through the conflicts, the misunderstandings, and the challenges that go with any relationship. As His Church, it is time to step into the maturity that will take on responsibility, to make sacrifices rather than live to please ourselves, and to persevere when things are tough. There is no "back door" on this relationship. Just as intended in human marriage on the earth, divorce is not an option. The choice is to choose to be changed and made right for the betterment of both involved.

Ephesians 4:15 exhorts us to no longer be children, but *"grow up into Him in all things"* (Eph. 4:15 KJV). Marriage provides the perfect platform for that to happen. Not only does it happen in the natural realm with our spouse but simultaneously with God in a spiritual realm.

God is not interested in marrying a "child bride." He is looking for His equal—as does a healthy marriage. He is looking for the mate who will bear the yoke with Him with excellence and zeal. Even though He always carries the greater weight of the yoke, our participation will make or break the movement forward.

Marriage helps us learn that life is no longer about "ourselves." To a two-year-old, the purpose of life is to get every need met. Everything is "mine, mine, mine." "Feed me!" "No!" "I want this, now!" This composes the deep realities of their childish vocabulary. For the maturing Christian, we evolve into considering one another more important than ourselves and *"giving preference to one another"* (see Phil. 2:3; Rom. 12:10 NKJV). We willingly *"lay down our lives"* (1 John 3:16 NKJV). Certainly, these lessons can be learned in other relationships, such as employer/employee, peers and siblings, et cetera. Yet your learning curve accelerates every day in marriage because of continuous contact, further trust and vulnerability, and greater opportunity for self-sacrifice.

LEAVING AND CLEAVING

For this reason a man shall leave his father and mother and shall be joined to his wife, and the two shall become one flesh (Ephesians 5:31 NKJV).

What exactly does a "leaving and cleaving" involve? In my understanding, your father and mother were your first natural means of support, provision, and protection. In that natural place where you were born, you were also trained.

Though you emerged from your mother's womb with both your father's and your mother's DNA, you are not and never will be "one" with them. You may share many similar traits—family resemblances or hereditary body types or propensities, hair or eye color, even talents or annoyances. You gained some sort of self-image in this context, for better or for worse. You learned conditional or perhaps unconditional love.

Yet in marriage things are changing, and God makes a very clear edict—leave and cleave. It appears to me that your old primary means of support, feedback, and image will be exchanged for something new. You and your mate will gain this as you grow together. (Hopefully, this is under God's tutelage and based on supernatural truths, not earthly observations.)

This mandate of "leave and cleave" seems to be a clarion call for a new beginning. The Word says you cannot serve two masters, lest you love one and hate the other (see Matt. 6:24). This can apply, too, in a spouse versus parent leadership role. While it in no way suggests cutting off family ties, it does suggest the primacy of the new role as the one in marriage for making ultimate decisions.

Cleaving is also a *mystery*, for the new union is unlike any previous relationship. Now you will lean on your mate (and God, as intended) in *every* way—body, soul, and spirit. I believe that just as in salvation, it is not something you can do without God's help. It requires faith and trust and God's blueprint to accomplish. It is supernatural in nature and requires making the shift from a "natural" way of doing and observing to a "supernatural" one.

Many marriages fail—even "Christian" ones—because they do not understand godly, supernatural covenant. Marriage is not just between a man and a woman, but between and man and a woman and God! God's perfection alone is the basis for stability and for the covenant to remain intact. We all fail each other, and probably most couples want to quit at some point. Yet it is God's grace, His enabling power, and *His side* of the bargain that makes it "do-able." Just as in salvation, I don't really believe "we find Jesus." I believe that, out of His love, He "finds us."

Similarly, we love in marriage because He first loved us. Our love is an act of our will that can continue even under the most adverse of conditions *when* it stems from His ability and favor—not our own. I believe this to be the same for us as His Corporate Bride.

A Place of Submission and Love

Too many false religions involve an acrid submission to some form of law, an idol, or a fallible man. There is nothing personal about it—rather, a "grit your teeth and do it" approach or else.

However, when God set up the order of the husband and wife in the Word, it is quite different. The husband does indeed have the final say. But this is in conjunction with the wife's active input and worth. It is done as an act of faith toward God first, then her husband. It is done respectfully for his position. The wife submits in faith, expecting that God will indeed empower the head to prosper from making right decisions for which he has also sought God's counsel.

You give your love and submission to the one who covers and protects you, not lessens or demands from you. In return, he is to love his wife as Christ loves the church (and, in earthly terms, as he loves himself). That means you are loved incomparably! That should change your view of yourself and your confidence.

The husband gives "his all" for his beloved and holds nothing back. Just as Jesus, he would give his own life if it was in her defense. He sees to her needs and cares for her with unselfish motives. The intent of his decisions is that which is pleasing to God and then beneficial to them both as a couple.

In macrocosm, let's look at this picture and consider our standing with the Lord.

We do not submit to the Lord as drones and follow him reluctantly. Nor do we simply or blindly follow him and hope for the best. Rather, we are His active and worthy partner, willingly pursuing Him and His dreams and having great faith and trust that His decisions are indeed best. He has not kept the wonder of His love or benefit silent or secret, as does some far-off deity. Rather, He has made known through the Word His kind intentions toward us day to day and throughout eternity. He loves us unconditionally just as we are.

We are His active and worthy partner, willingly pursuing Him and His dreams and having great faith and trust that His decisions are indeed best.

It is not hard or unbefitting to submit yourself to such a husband. Rather, it is fulfilling and right to do so. Our hearts are gladdened and secure from this holy place, and order is set that benefits both. It is our honor to forever be His corporate Bride.

Do You Take This Man?

In the end, the "mystery" still involves free will decisions. Will you be His Bride?

Consider the gaze of Jesus at the altar waiting for us. Look at the intensity and pleasure in His gaze. There are no distractions. Jesus has eyes for us only. He has a right to know that we, as His Bride, have the same sole focus.

In this life, it suggests that our mate wants and merits our love and attention. It cannot be replaced by a television dinner or a ball game, for a mate wants intimate conversation and life exchange with us as their beloved. So does Jesus.

As in an earthly romance, there is jealousy and tension when rightful attention is not given. We know that we can rely on Jesus to be faithful to us. We stand in the secure position that He has already paid the price of His very blood for the permission of having our hand in marriage.

Yet what is our position toward Him? Are we easily attracted to other things—things of this world, the lust of the eye, the lust of the flesh, and the boastful pride of life? Are we given to Him wholly, knowing that we are *"bought at a price,"* and that our bodies are not our own? (See 1 Cor. 6:19-20 NKJV.) Do we belong to Him in worship, service, and loving action? Is His love safe with us?

I believe Jesus created intimacy with Him as our deepest desire because true love is irresistible. It beats out all contenders. It is the highest satisfaction and fulfillment possible to us naturally and spiritually.

Idol worship, on the other hand, is not. We tire of idols, they disappoint us, and we move on. This could be jobs, entertainments, money, or false religion to name a few. Yet we still must choose to whom or what we will be married.

God has created us with a place in our body, soul, and spirit that is only completed by intimacy. This is not to say all must marry in this age. The apostle Paul makes it clear in the Word that this is not the case.

However, the capacity and desire for intimacy is still a part of every one of us—hence the ability and openness to give ourselves fully to our Bridegroom whether or not we marry on this earth. For only in that spiritual union can we fully enjoy that for which we were created.

THE FINAL REWARD

When the Lord chose the mystery of marriage to parallel His relationship with the Church, He was well aware of our limitations as spiritual human beings to communicate our emotions. On this earth, most would consider the union of a man and a woman in marriage to be the deepest and most ultimate way to express and enjoy love as one. Yet this may not be the whole picture. As minister Tommy Tenney observed at a conference I attended, "Most of us see ourselves as *human* beings living a *temporary spiritual existence*. But the truth is that we are *spiritual* beings living a *temporary human existence*."

What does this mean? I believe one of the answers is found in Matthew 22 where we read that in Heaven, *"They neither marry nor are given in marriage"* (Matt. 22:30 NASB). If this is such a wonderful estate here and now, then why would it be denied in Heaven?

I believe it is because in the presence of the Lord we will each be totally fulfilled spirit beings. We will have higher ways of communication and understanding that far surpass even the best relationship we could experience now.

No doubt earthly unions will pale in comparison when we will look into His eyes and find ourselves knowing as we have been fully known (see 1 Cor. 13:12). As the final veil of death and the struggles of humanity are removed, we shall be fully like Him, for we shall see Him as He is! (See 1 John 3:2.) No doubt, we shall also be fully *one with Him and each other in spirit* in an all-knowing, all-seeing, all-understanding, and highly satisfied way.

That, my friend, is the ultimate reward—and surely one mystery solved!

CHAPTER 2

The Irresistible Grace of God

SAM HINN

Mike stood in the pew unable to accept the pastor's altar call. The heaviness in his legs matched the feeling that his feet were nailed to the carpeted floor. Despite the powerful message he had just heard and the desire in his heart to meet the Lord at the altar, Mike couldn't gather the courage to move.

Others were running to the altar, many with tears streaming down their face. Some were screaming. Mike figured they would be hoarse in a matter of minutes. He longed for either of those expressions of joy. He couldn't remember the last time he cried or laughed. He hung his head as the tug in his heart grew.

The pastor continued to shout encouragement to those still in their seats. "C'mon! Don't be afraid." He looked right at Mike. "The

Lord wants to meet you down here. Take that step." The pastor moved across the stage as people poured out of the pews to fill the aisles leading to the altar. "It's not about you. It's not about your love for Him. It's about His love for you."

Oh Lord, I am not worthy. How you can You forgive me for what I have done? I am a horrible person. I have sinned far too many sins. I have walked away from You more times than I can count. I want to go, but I can't.

The small whisper in Mike's heart startled him. He immediately recognized the Lord's voice: "But you can."

Instead, Mike slumped down into the pew and buried his head in his hands. He sat for a long time without moving. The pastor's plea continued to boom over the speakers, rattling the stained-glass windows. He finally leaned back in his seat. A tear formed in the corner of his eye and rolled slowly down his cheek.

Mike's inner turmoil is not uncommon in the church today. Too many times the churchgoer, even a long-time Christian, struggles with the perception of not being good enough in God's eyes. That's because many Americans are raised being told such things as, "You get what you deserve in life," "If you want to make something of your life, it's up to you," and the widely popular, "If it is to be, it's up to me."

What horrible mantras to live by.

These words and phrases cause people to operate in a works mentality. So they live under the presumption that they get what they deserve, particularly when they have sinned. However, the Bible says God is a gracious God. That means He loves to be gracious to you. God loves to bless people who don't deserve it. Think for a moment of the last time that you received something that you didn't deserve.

We can't earn grace. God gives us grace. (See Psalms 145:8-9.) Grace is something that God gives us that we don't deserve. This is not to be confused with mercy, which is God *not* giving us something that we *do* deserve. For example, if a police officer pulls you over for speeding and gives you a warning without a ticket, then you just received mercy. That is, you were forgiven and you did not receive the punishment due you. But that is not grace. If the police officer gave you the warning and then, instead of handing you a ticket, he gave you a gift of one thousand dollars, then you just received grace.

When you understand grace, completely grasp the depth of it, you'll feel closer to God than you ever have in your life.

You can't understand the Christian life at all unless you understand grace. It's at the heart of our faith. When you understand grace, completely grasp the depth of it, you'll feel closer to God than you ever have in your life. You'll be more drawn to Him, love Him more, and be more grateful. It's by grace that God brings us to Him. Romans 5:17 says,

> *For if by the one man's offense death reigned through the one, much more those who receive abundance of grace and of the gift of righteousness will reign in life through the One, Jesus Christ* (Romans 5:17 NKJV).

To live in grace, we must first walk away from the law. But the enemy wants nothing more than for you to live by the law and to beat yourself up for him. The devil knows that the moment you receive a revelation of God's love and His grace for your life it will be one of your greatest freedoms in Christ.

Keeping the law sounds commendable. Contrary to what most of us have heard in church for years, attempting to follow the law, and nothing but the law, is not intended to draw us closer to God.

> For as by one man's disobedience many were made sinners, so also by one Man's obedience many will be made righteous. Moreover the law entered that the offense might abound. But where sin abounded, grace abounded much more (Romans 5:19-20 NKJV).

> Therefore by the deeds of the law no flesh will be justified in His sight, for by the law is the knowledge of sin (Romans 3:20 NKJV).

The law was given so man could see the condition of his relationship with God. Under the law, we must be perfect, holy, and righteous. But the law shows just how imperfect, unholy, and unrighteous we really are. We are condemned by our faults, our guilt, and our sins. (See John 1:17.) We aren't meant to live by the law. That ended when Jesus died on the Cross. Despite the grace of God, many still want to live under the law. Think of it this way—the law was then, and this is now.

What we need is a revelation of how much God loves us. This revelation will transform our lives. First John 4:10-11 says:

> In this is love, not that we loved God, but that He loved us and sent His Son to be the propitiation for our sins. Beloved,

if God so loved us, we also ought to love one another (1 John 4:10-11 NKJV).

Now, let's examine three things we receive with this revelation.

FOCUS ON GOD'S LOVE FOR YOU, NOT YOUR LOVE FOR HIM

I have been crucified with Christ; it is no longer I who live, but Christ lives in me; and the life which I now live in the flesh I live by faith in the Son of God, who loved me and gave Himself for me. I do not set aside the grace of God; for if righteousness comes through the law, then Christ died in vain (Galatians 2:20-21 NKJV).

In this Scripture, Paul put his eyes not on his love for God, but rather God's love for him. When we put our eyes on our love for Him, it will do any number of things—vary, fluctuate, go up and down. God's love for us, however, is constant and steady. His love never changes. There is absolutely nothing you can do to change the depth of His love for you. No amount of spiritual aerobics, no matter what you give up to follow Christ, no amount of biblical knowledge, conferences, or prophetic meetings can make God love you any more than He loves you right now.

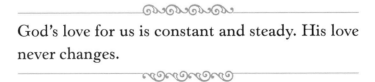

God's love for us is constant and steady. His love never changes.

Remember the thief who hung on the cross next to Christ on Golgotha. That thief confessed out of fear that day. He never studied the Bible, never set foot in a synagogue, and never made things right with the people he wronged, yet he asked, *"Jesus, remember me."* To which Jesus replied, *"Today you will be with Me in paradise."* (See Luke 23:42-43.)

This is a perfect reminder that grace does not depend on what we have done for God, but rather what God does, and can do, for us.

SPIRITUAL GROWTH

Early on the first day of the week, while it was still dark, Mary Magdalene went to the tomb and saw that the stone had been removed from the entrance. So she came running to Simon Peter and the other disciple, the one Jesus loved, and said, "They have taken the Lord out of the tomb, and we don't know where they have put Him!" So Peter and the other disciple started for the tomb. Both were running, but the other disciple outran Peter and reached the tomb first (John 20:1-4).

No matter your age or how long you have been walking with God, your spiritual growth is attached to God's love for you and not your love for Him. Today most Christians realize that they do not have to keep all of the Old Testament Laws, but now we have our own set of laws. If you really want to grow in God, let Him love you. Let Him touch your heart with His grace and not your works. This is a key moment for us as we transition from us loving Him to Him loving us.

SPIRITUAL INSIGHT

When Jesus had said these things, He was troubled in spirit, and testified and said, "Most assuredly, I say to you, one of you will betray Me." Then the disciples looked at one another, perplexed about whom He spoke. Now there was leaning on Jesus' bosom one of His disciples, whom Jesus loved. Simon Peter therefore motioned to him to ask who it was of whom He spoke. Then, leaning back on Jesus' breast, he said to Him, "Lord, who is it?" Jesus answered, "It is he to whom I shall give a piece of bread when I have dipped it." And having dipped the bread, He gave it to Judas Iscariot, the son of Simon (John 13:21-26 NKJV).

This expression "the disciple whom Jesus loved" is only found in the book of John, and it shows up five times in his writings.

On the night that Jesus was betrayed, it says John was leaning on Jesus' chest. He was not relying and depending on his love for the Lord, but the Lord's love for him. Peter, on the other hand, typifies the believers who are always boasting about their love for the Lord, but he was the one who denied Jesus three times. It was Peter who said to Jesus, "I will never betray You; they can all betray You but not me."

So much of our walk with God and the focus of the church has been on us loving God. There is so much preaching about how to love God. How many times have you heard the message "You've got to love God more," or "How to fall in love with God"?

Enough already.

It is not enough to receive just mercy. It is not enough to believe that our sins are forgiven. We must posture ourselves under God's blessings that constantly flow from Heaven.

By not understanding the difference, many continue to live under the power of sin and death while pleading for God's mercy. Of course, God forgives them for these sins because He is a merciful God. Those who would only access the mercy of God are missing out. It is not enough to receive just mercy. It is not enough to believe that our sins are forgiven. We must posture ourselves under God's blessings which constantly flow from Heaven. We must receive it into our very life. Only then will we reign in life.

We strive for power over sin. We want to reign over sin—that's why we often go back to the law. It's easy to understand and follow. It's black and white. But it doesn't work. You can't keep doing something the same way over and over and expect a different result. So let's try something different.

Think of yourself as a tree for a moment. Trees stand vertically, spreading out their branches, allowing the sun and rain to bathe them. They do not strive to produce fruit and that fruit just comes forth automatically. The more sun, nutrients, and water they receive, the more fruit a tree will produce. Trees know how to receive, and in that receiving, they declare to man the relationship God maintains with all of His creation.

We need to be like that tree—drinking in God's grace. It is God's favor, power, and nature being poured out on your behalf. If you want to reign in life, you must receive an "abundance" of this grace. Be thirsty, needy, and desirous for God's grace to flow into you. It is available free and abundant.

When a Christian lives under grace, he discovers power that enables and causes him to fulfill God's will. We discover:

- Grace is greater than our sin.

- Grace is wonderful, but sometimes our sin will still carry consequences.

- Don't take God's grace for granted and do what you please.

- Grace reigns through righteousness.

I know many of you probably think you understand grace. You are saved by grace. You've known that for many years. But I've discovered that even many Christians, although they know they're saved by grace, sure don't act like it. In fact, they spend most of their life thinking and acting like we're saved by works.

You cannot overcome or remove your habits on your own will power or positive thinking. But God's amazing grace will give you the power you need to overcome every bad habit in your life. And in doing so, you will receive two great gifts—the abundance of grace and the gift of righteousness. These gifts will help you to reign in life. When you reign in life, you reign over all your habits.

To provide freedom from and victory over the power of sin and death, God sent Jesus. This is what Paul wanted the Christians in Rome and you and me to understand. As sin and death came through Adam, grace and life came through Jesus Christ. (See Romans 5:12-17.)

All who have put their faith in Jesus have experienced an initial burst of grace which brought us into forgiveness and a relationship with God. But few have come to a revelation concerning how that power which flows through Jesus can be experienced on a consistent, ongoing basis.

My prayer for each of you is that God would reveal His amazing grace to you, so that the next time a pastor is encouraging people to join him at the altar you can lock arms with Mike and head to the front.

CHAPTER 3

Intimacy With God: Catching His Heart for Others

CHRISTY WIMBER

I think my young son, John, said it best when I asked him, "If Jesus was standing in front of you right now, what do you think He would say to you?"

He didn't even hesitate, saying, "He would say, I am here to protect you, and I will stand up to anybody that would want to hurt you."

I thought, *You know, if we all felt like that, I think it would change the way we approach our Heavenly Father.* If you know your Father is there for you—in a sense, that He has your back—then of course you would tell Him everything. Of course He would be the first One you and I would run too no matter what we're facing.

INTIMACY IN AND THROUGH US

One of the greatest promises you and I have is that He always sees us not as we are, but as we will and should be. He is your greatest fan; He is the one that will always be faithful to the end of the ages. He is the one that loves you and never ignores you when you cry for help (see Isa. 30:19).

But there's always so much more involved with intimacy than we realize. Do you feel like God has your back? Do you feel like He is the safest place for you? How you answer those two questions will pretty much tell you how much intimacy you have with the Father.

No true transaction of intimacy takes place between people unless trust is involved. Only when I trust someone am I able to open my heart in a vulnerable and transparent way. Trust is at the core of intimacy with our relationships we have around us in our daily lives, as well as with the Lord.

One way to really know what you trust is to ask yourself the question, "What do I run to when I get great or horrible news?" Do you call a friend? Your spouse? Do you run to the bar or to the fridge? What you rely on is what you trust in because we're called to trust in Him, and we show we're trusting Him when we're leaning on Him, meaning to find refuge. (See Proverbs 3:5.)

Trust can be such a huge issue for people, but trusting is the key to intimacy. People are dying all around us for the kind of intimacy Jesus desires to have with you and I. And I don't just mean people that aren't saved—I mean people in the church. Too many people know about God—in fact, they even know all the right actions and traditions—yet they don't know Him on a deep, personal level.

Do you know the Father not just by what you do, but from who you are? I think it's important to ask ourselves that question. I know I can do many things for God, and I know it moves His heart to know I love doing His Kingdom work, but I also know that at the end of the day, what my King wants out of me is just that—*me*. He wants intimate relationship with Christy. The King wants you.

I find it interesting how important intimacy is with the Lord, since He created us to have a deep relationship with Him as well as with each other. And, only when we're in touch with the One who created every aspect of who we are, are we really able to understand who we truly are in Christ and all He has for us.

What my King wants out of me is just that—*me*. He wants intimate relationship with Christy. The King wants you.

If I don't really know how God sees me, then how can I extend that offer to others? How can I model that to others, unless there's such a difference in me because I am being touched and seen over and over again by the One who made me? It's when He sees me and I know He sees me, yet I feel safe.

I still believe that at the end of the day He is still the safest place for me—He is my protector. He is the one who will always have my back.

Look at the story of the woman at the well in John 4. It wasn't just that Jesus spoke to her—it was that He saw what everyone else couldn't. He spoke to her heart. He spoke into the heart of who she really was. How many times do you think she walked around town and the people spoke behind her back? How many times do you think she heard the people whisper loudly even though she was present? How many times do you think she felt the stares of judgment all around her?

Jesus cut through all that and told her how it was, but in a way that spoke directly to her heart. Not with judgment, but in a way of seeing the real her. If Jesus would have spoken to her in a judgmental sort of way, her response would have been much different. Her response would have been more defensive, or she would have said nothing and run.

Yet Jesus saw past the sin to see the sinner, in such an intimate way that spoke directly to her heart. There was a transaction that took place that was so intimate that she was taken aback. Her sin wasn't a "turn-off" to Jesus; He knew who she was and what she was about. In fact, He even knew what others would think of Him because He was speaking to her. Just the fact that they were alone talking could have started more gossip. Yet it didn't seem to bother Jesus a bit.

And the good news? Our sin isn't a turn-off to Jesus, either! All we have to do is look at the Scriptures and who Jesus had around Him. The people that Jesus picked to carry on the church were so messed up. None of them went to seminary or had great reputations. Most of them were ordinary people that no one else would have picked to come on their team.

But not Jesus. He chose the thief, the tax collector, and the guys that fished for a living. He chose the people that others didn't seem to really acknowledge or particularly like. But when He spoke, it hit them at the core of who they were, so that they were ready to drop everything just to follow this Man. Just to have relationship with this Jesus.

If we look at how Jesus always saw the difference between the person and whatever "sin" they might have done, I think we could catch the very heart of God, not only for ourselves, but also for those around us. I think we get too scared of sin. However, it didn't seem to bother Jesus much; He still chose to talk to, eat with, and fellowship on intimate levels with those that didn't have it all together. And in turn, they were the ones that invited him in—they wanted to be with this Man called Jesus. The invitation is always what moves the heart of Jesus.

In pastoring, I've found too many people don't talk to God much, mostly because of shame. We tend to go to God about surface stuff— what financial need we might have, what we're worried about at the time, what we need some faith for at the time. Yet in Romans it talks about the Holy Spirit needing to intercede on our behalf because most of the time we aren't even in touch with what our real needs are.

True intimacy comes where He sees into who we really are. There's that connection that takes place, that fills a void in us—"our deep calling to His deep" (See Psalms 42:7.)

Too many people are afraid of intimacy because they're afraid of being "found out." I mean, we do that in relationships all the time. Scared to be the real us, feeling that if we do then the person won't really like us or want to be our friend. But true intimacy comes when we share the deepest parts of who we are and the person loves us even more for sharing.

Remember Abraham, who was called "a friend of God"? And really, why was that? They spoke face to face. There were exchanges that took place.

Oftentimes, people think that anyone knowing their heart is too scary. So, most interaction is the usual, "How are you?"

"Good. And you?"

"I'm fine."

"How's work?"

"Good."

"Well, tell your family hello. See you later!"

Doesn't that sound familiar? This sort of surface interaction is how we tend to communicate much of the time.

In my own life I've found it's easy for me in my intimate relationship with others to be too worried about what they can do to hurt me. So, to be vulnerable is to put myself in a place where I can be ruined. It seems like too much of a risk at times. It would be much easier for me just to have my intimacy with the Father, in fact, it would be a lot easier at times! But in order for God to take me to another level of trust, I have to be able to trust those He also sends into my life. It's just part of it.

I've found that in my intimate times with the Lord, He shows me where to go. He shows me those He himself is bringing into my life, and I have a choice whether or not I will trust Him through that process. But every time it seems to take me to a deeper level of trust and intimacy with Him. I know that even if no one sticks by me—even if I am betrayed or hurt in some way—I will still have the Lord.

Spending time with God is never just about us and the Father. It's always for those around us, too. What happens in me—God's Kingdom in me—is what creates His Kingdom around me. Everything I learn from the Father is for a reason. There are things He wants to show me that will only come when it's just He and I.

I mean, look at Jesus, our model of prayer, who went to go be with the Father. It wasn't just to be encouraged and to get filled up again, it was also to know the Father's heart and plan for those Jesus was around. So Jesus knew what the Father's heart was for the people. Remember, Jesus could only do whatever the Father showed Him (see John 5:19).

You and I will not be able to catch God's heart for those around us unless we catch it for ourselves first. We must see the bigger picture as to why He wants to move in us and around us. God cannot do through you what He hasn't done in you first.

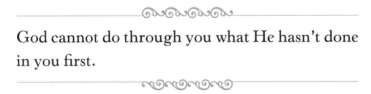

God cannot do through you what He hasn't done in you first.

See, I think when we talk about intimacy with the Father, we have to be able to catch His heart for others in a way where we are able to get past all the junk in people's lives. Where through you and I we have an intimate encounter with the Lord Himself. Where all we're doing is being the midwife, in a sense. Where we're just part of the transaction, however, we don't feel the need to make it about ourselves, but rather are able to show the people how to connect to the Father. How He really loves and sees who they are, not just what they may have done.

If we don't catch the intimacy the Father has for us, then it's too difficult to be able to see that for others. At the end of the day, I know that many won't be able to see who the person of Christy is, but I do know that my intimacy with the Father is what makes it possible for me to see that for others. It doesn't take a genius or a prophetic gifting to see what's wrong with people. However, it takes some real courage, effort, and risk to be able to see people the way Christ does.

People don't need us; they need the God in us. You can never overestimate the power of your intimacy with Christ. Never is it a waste of time, and never is it just for us.

One thing I've learned throughout the years is for me, the safest place is my time just between God and me. How He uses that is up to Him. But I know that every time I'm with Him, He causes me to see things the way He does. He gives me His heart for people, and without intimacy it would be impossible.

I really love being around people at times that have no idea of who God is. I love it that they don't know how to talk, walk, or dress "Christianese." It doesn't bother me a bit. I mean, how do they know unless someone reaches out to share and be another option?

My husband and I were at his work party not long ago, which was quite interesting but we had a great time. But why we had such a great time is that we got to hang out with people that don't know the Lord yet. One guy walked up to us and said, "Now I know you're religious, so forgive me for my *%^%#* language."

So I said to him, "Well, I'm not religious, but I am a pastor."

And this guy just looked at me with the funniest face and responded by saying, "Well, how the heck do you do that?"

I love people's responses to something nonreligious. I think it's so great to see people around us get an encouraging message that doesn't have to do with something they may be doing wrong with their life. In fact, I think it's important as believers that we're out offering the same message that someone went out of their way to offer to us.

One of the most powerful witnessing tools for me is hearing the Father's heart for someone I'm talking to. Asking the question, "Lord, what would You like to say to this person today?" People aren't expecting some encouraging word for nothing, and in my opinion the gift of encouragement is the most under-used spiritual gift! And the amazing thing is, anyone can do it!

Just like you and I need to know we're OK. Just like you and I need to be encouraged—how much more do the people around you need it? The ones that have no other hope than what they can find in themselves.

See your ability to open up to the Father. To catch His heart for you is what He's after. But in those times of intimacy with Him, He will begin to show you things for those around you that will not only change their lives, but it will take you to a deeper level of your walk with Jesus.

Surrender your heart to Jesus in a way that you're learning to "find refuge" in Him, trusting Him with all you are. Learn to trust Him in a way that you know He is the safest place to be. That when all is said and done, without hesitation, you know God has your back. That He is your great Protector!

CHAPTER 4

The Crowning Glory of Our Lives
S.J. HILL

Every one of us came into the world wanting to feel special to someone. This human longing is something we all share. It is an innate desire that we have carried with us from birth. Yet many of us have grown up not knowing what it is to feel valued and treasured by even those closest to us. The dull ache of rejection and loneliness still haunts us as we try to carve out a niche for ourselves in the grand scheme of life.

Like a cruel taskmaster, the need for significance has driven us to find our worth in our accomplishments or in the approval of others. Some of us have gone to great lengths to try to satisfy this longing. We've become masters at *playing the game* in order to be successful and to win the acceptance of our peers. But, in reality, all we have ended up doing is getting caught on a carousel that never seems to stop.

Recently, I watched an interview of Hillary Clinton conducted by a news reporter. Mrs. Clinton was being asked about her childhood and some of the factors that had made her a highly motivated individual. She admitted that one of the reasons why she is such a driven person is because of the way she was raised by her father. She reminisced about coming home from school on one occasion, excited to show her dad her report card. When he saw that she had gotten an A- in one particular class, instead of praising her and affirming her for her effort, all he could say was, "Why didn't you get an A?" Does Hillary Clinton's experience sound all too familiar?

One of my closest friends is in the American Motorcycle Association Hall of Fame. Steve was inducted into the Hall in 2001. He is the only biker to win the AMA Motocross, the AMA Supercross, and the AMA Superbike nationals. In 1982, he was voted by the American Motorcycle Association as their Professional Athlete of the Year. Steve will always be considered one of the most multitalented riders in the history of motorcycle racing.

Yet Steve struggled for years with a deep-seated insecurity rooted in a nagging sense of insignificance. Looking at his accomplishments in and out of racing, you would have never known it. Steve has also owned a successful real estate investment company and has been involved in a fruitful Christian ministry as well. Still, he never truly felt successful.

Like a lot of us, Steve grew up not experiencing the loving acceptance and affirmation of his earthly father. His dad was "old school," believing that the best way to motivate his son was by making him think he couldn't do anything good enough. Steve worked hard at motorcycle racing in order to *win* the approval of his father, but he never got it. On the day when Steve was inducted into the Hall of Fame, his dad didn't even tell him he was proud of him.

It wasn't until several years ago that Steve began to understand and experience the wonderful acceptance and affirmation of a greater Father who loved him more than any earthly father ever could. Although the wounds and pain of the past still trouble him at times, Steve is slowly coming to a place of wholeness that he has never known before.

Stories like Steve's are all too common. I hear them everywhere I go. These "father issues" seem to plague the human race. Several years ago, I was teaching at a conference near Brisbane, Australia. I was talking about the Father's love and His extravagant affections for us. A couple of days after the conference, I was introduced to a very successful businessman who had attended the meetings. He admitted to me that he was having a hard time embracing some of the things I had taught because it was difficult for him to believe that God really liked him and enjoyed him for who he was. He proceeded to tell me that he had been raised by a father who, throughout his life, had repeatedly told him he wouldn't amount to anything. As I looked at this man and listened to his story, my heart went out to him. I instinctively knew that he had worked overtime at being successful just to prove his "old man" wrong.

In a perfect world, the family unit and fathers in particular were to be a reflection of God's unfailing love for His children.

In a perfect world, the family unit and fathers in particular were to be a reflection of God's unfailing love for His children. But in a fallen world infected by sin, the vicious cycle of rejection has been repeated over and over again. Fathers have passed down to their sons and daughters the pain inflicted on them from early childhood. In turn, the cruel words, clenched fists, and callous indifference of dads have ended up crippling children in every generation.

Today, absent fathers (physically and emotionally), abusive fathers, and addicted fathers have created huge problems for societies around the world. For example, in America, 90 percent of all runaway children come from fatherless homes. Three out of four teenage suicides occur as a result of fatherless environments. Children from fatherless homes are twice as likely to be high school dropouts, and girls are three times more likely to become unwed teenage mothers. Furthermore, 70 percent of all men in prison also come from fatherless homes.

The rampant results of rejection are staggering. The pain of being unwanted and the sense of despair over feeling unloved seem to have a stranglehold on humanity. Loneliness has reached epidemic proportions as man's search for significance continues.

In *The Way to Love*, Anthony DeMello wrote:

> Look at your life and see how you have filled its emptiness with people. As a result they have a strangle hold on you. See how they control your behavior by their approval and disapproval. They hold the power to ease your loneliness with their company, to send your spirits soaring with their praise, to bring you down to the depths with their criticism and rejection. Take a look at yourself spending

almost every waking moment of your day placating and pleasing people, whether they are living or dead. You live by their norms, conform to their standards, seek their company, desire their love, dread their ridicule, long for their applause, meekly submit to the guilt they lay upon you; you are terrified to go against the fashion in the way you dress or speak or act or even think. And observe how even when you control them you depend on them and are enslaved by them. People have become so much a part of your being that you cannot even imagine living a life that is unaffected or uncontrolled by them.[1]

While the symptoms of rejection may vary in different individuals, the underlying cause is deeply embedded in feelings of insignificance. Teenagers will embrace the latest fashion trends and behavioral patterns of their peers just to feel accepted. Girls will become sexually promiscuous just because they long for the love and affection they didn't receive from their fathers. The desire to feel attractive and special to someone often causes them to confuse sex for love. And young men will strive to become the latest and greatest sports jocks just to win the approval of their fathers and the praise of their peers.

A student of mine recently admitted that it has been hard for him to freely receive the unconditional love of his heavenly Father. What has been the underlying cause? The people who were supposed to love and nurture him as a child ended up hurting him the most. His dad used to tell him that he was stupid, and his school grades took a downward spiral as a result. He so wanted his father's approval that he poured all of his energy into basketball. He became such a good player that he eventually was voted team captain by his peers. Yet his father didn't seem to care and never attended any of his games. Even when he graduated from high school, his dad was conspicuously absent from the ceremony. This young man grew up believing that he really wasn't worth anyone's time and attention, even God's.

As adults, we can also find ourselves continually searching for significance in the things we do and in the people we know. It can easily become "second nature" for us to measure our worth by the cars we drive, the degrees on our walls, the homes in which we live, the positions we hold, the relationships we've embraced, the recognition of others, and the size of our savings accounts and our stock portfolios. We can readily deceive ourselves into believing that success of any kind will bring us happiness and fulfillment, but it never does. The emptiness we inevitably experience only reminds us that we can never do enough to really gain the approval of others or to feel good about ourselves.

We can readily deceive ourselves into believing that success of any kind will bring us happiness and fulfillment, but it never does.

This emptiness has been a part of the human dilemma ever since man chose to believe satan's lie. Sin left a gaping hole in the hearts of men and women, and with it came a gnawing sense of loneliness that has tormented the human race from nearly the beginning of time.

It was into this dark abyss of human existence that Jesus would be born. The sting of rejection would play no favorites even when it came to the Son of God. From His birth, Jesus was rumored to be an illegitimate child of a delusional teenage girl. The Bible also suggests that there was nothing physically attractive about Him as well (see Isa. 53:2). Members of His own family didn't believe in Him until after His resurrection from the dead and, if that wasn't bad enough, He was called a drunkard and a glutton. Religious leaders suspected that he was demonized, and bystanders called him terrible names. He was also rejected by those He loved, deemed a loser, and crucified as a criminal.

THE FATHER'S LOVING APPROVAL

Yet, what enabled Jesus to cope with the emotional trauma that seemed to follow Him like a shadow throughout His life? He lived out of the *loving approval* of His heavenly Father. As a man living in a world polluted with pain, it was imperative for Jesus to be affirmed by His Father. This is why Abba, in a booming voice, spoke these powerful words over His Son at His baptism: *"You are My beloved Son; in You I am well pleased"* (Luke 3:22 NKJV).

Think of it. The Father's affirmation was the most decisive moment in Jesus' life up to that point. His *true identity* was declared to Him, and this was how He began His ministry in Galilee. Before He had healed one person, cast out one demon, preached one sermon, or multiplied food like popcorn, He experienced both a personal and profound affirmation from His Father. But the words of Abba were not based on anything He had done; instead, they were deeply rooted in the reality that He was uniquely loved by His heavenly Father and had a very special relationship with Him. The supreme passion in Jesus' life was His Father. This would be the key to His success in life and ministry.

In Isaiah 42:1-4, we find a prophetic proclamation concerning Messiah that parallels the powerful affirmation given to Jesus by His Father:

> *Behold! My Servant whom I uphold, My Elect One in whom My soul delights! I have put My Spirit upon Him; He will bring forth justice to the Gentiles. He will not cry out, nor raise His voice, nor cause His voice to be heard in the street. A bruised reed He will not break, and smoking flax He will not quench; He will bring forth justice for truth. He will not fail nor be discouraged, till He has established justice in the earth; and the coastlands shall wait for His law* (Isaiah 42:1-4 NKJV).

This passage also reinforces the impact the Father's affirmation and approval would have on His Son. According to verse 2, Messiah wouldn't have to *"...cry out nor raise His voice, nor cause His voice to be heard in the street"* to try to gain men's attention and approval. He wouldn't have to satisfy His own ego through self-promotion, because His Father's loving care and affirmation would bring fulfillment to His life and keep Him from needing any false comfort from men.

Isaiah also predicted Messiah wouldn't have to prove His authority through the abuse and control of others. *"A bruised reed He will not break, and smoking flax He will not quench"* (Isa. 42:3 NKJV). Because Jesus' security and identity would be established in His Father's love, He wouldn't have to go out of His way to appear powerful by extinguishing the fire that was barely burning in the lives of individuals that He could just as easily have despised.

It was further promised in verse three that Messiah *"...will bring forth justice for truth."* Because Jesus would live out of the Father's approval, He wouldn't have to be subject to religious expediency or build His ministry on political correctness. This is why He would be able to truthfully confront the religious system of His day, as he exposed the hypocrisy and corruption that existed in the hearts of its leaders.

Isaiah also prophesied that Messiah *"...will not fail nor be discouraged, till He has established justice in the earth"* (Isa. 42:4 NKJV). Discouragement would not be able to overwhelm Jesus because He would consciously live in His Father's delight. Because Christ would be grounded in His Father's affections, His focus would remain steadfast until His ministry was fulfilled.

Yet things would be anything but easy for the promised Messiah. Although Jesus grew up perfectly adjusted emotionally because of the love of His Father, His Sonship would continually be called into question. Even after hearing the powerful affirmation of His Father at His baptism, Jesus found Himself in the desert tempted by satan. The devil challenged Him to *prove* His Sonship by turning stones into bread, throwing Himself from the pinnacle of the temple to be caught by angels, and by embracing the prominence and prestige that would be due Him in accepting the offer of the kingdoms of the world. But Jesus resisted the temptations of success, popularity, and power by living out of His true identity. Jesus didn't have to prove to those around Him that He was worthy of love. In fact, He didn't have to prove anything because He was already the "Beloved of the Father," and that allowed Him to live free from the persuasive ploys of the Enemy.

A number of years ago I had the privilege of ministering for two weekends in the New Orleans, Louisiana, area. I had some time off between meetings, and so I retreated to a secluded place that had been provided for me where I could rest and reflect on some things I had been reading. I was specifically drawn to two passages in the Gospel of John. For several days, I found myself visiting these verses again and again. It was as if I was on a pilgrimage and the Holy Spirit had prepared a place of solitude for me so He could speak to me about something that would change my life and the way I would approach ministry.

With John as my companion, I set out on the journey and found myself intrigued by two verses he had written in his Gospel—John 13:23 and John 21:20. While they appear to be very similar in nature, together they reiterate a truth that is essential for our emotional and spiritual well-being. In speaking of himself, John writes, *"Now there was leaning on Jesus' bosom one of His disciples, whom Jesus loved"* (John 13:23 NKJV). In John 21:20, he further states that *"Peter, turning around, saw the disciple whom Jesus loved following, who also had leaned on His breast at the supper..."* (John 21:20 NKJV). Notice, in both instances John referred to himself as *"the disciple whom Jesus loved."*

John understood that he was special to the One who is able to love each of us as if we were His favorite.

John often spoke of having a special, unique relationship with Christ. In fact, on three other occasions he makes reference to being *"the disciple whom Jesus loved"* (John 19:26; 20:2; 21:7 NKJV). It may appear that John was being a bit egotistical about his close connection with Christ but, in reality that was not the case at all. John wasn't suggesting that he was better than the other disciples. Instead, he was speaking out of a personal revelation he had experienced about the all-encompassing, superior love of God. *John understood that he was special to the One who is able to love each of us as if we were His favorite.*

If you could have asked John, "What is your core identity and from what do you draw your significance?" he would have never replied, "I am an apostle, a minister, a miracle-worker." He would have simply said, "I am the one Jesus loves." John understood that he was God's favorite. He knew he was special, not because of his accomplishments in ministry, but because of who loved him. He was the "beloved of the Father" and that became his *true identity* and the crowning glory of his life.

This was the truth the Holy Spirit wanted to instill in my heart and mind during my brief retreat. I was being invited to embrace my core identity as Abba's special son, but the concept was somewhat difficult for me to grasp. For years, I had struggled with a deep sense of insignificance. I was often lonely growing up and wondered why I had to initiate getting together with the kids in my neighborhood. It was experiences like these that reinforced the rejection I felt and led me to believe that there had to be something wrong with me.

Even after I had been in ministry for some time, I was still haunted by periods of incredible loneliness. I would wonder why I didn't receive more phone calls from the people I had met in my travels whom I had come to love and appreciate. Why was I the one who had to make the calls and pursue the relationships? I also struggled at times with questions about why I wasn't receiving more invitations to travel and minister, and I battled with thoughts that questioned my speaking ability.

There were also occasions when I would watch Christian television and catch myself comparing my ministry to others and wonder why God was seemingly using them more than me. I felt insignificant even to God, and I couldn't understand why He wouldn't give me more opportunities to serve Him. No, it wasn't about having my ego stroked; it was about the rejection I felt and the deep-seated pain I had carried for years.

These were the issues the Holy Spirit was lovingly confronting during my time in Louisiana. I knew He was exposing certain mindsets and emotional wounds, not to shame me but to enable me to live free as His son. He wanted me to know that as much as He loved the things I had done for Him, He delighted in me solely because of who He had made me to be for Himself. My *worth* was not based on my ministry accomplishments, but instead on the fact that I was the "beloved of the Father."

It was then that I truly understood our success in the Christian life does not primarily consist of what we do for our Father but what our Father has done for us—the incomprehensible things He has dreamed up and accomplished for us through His Son, Jesus Christ.

Success in the Kingdom of God is not ultimately determined by one's accomplishments; true success is based on the understanding that we are infinitely loved and cherished by God. It is living and serving out of the reality that we have been called and chosen to be lovers of God.

This life-changing truth is further reflected in Psalms: *"You give me Your shield of victory, and Your right hand sustains me; You stoop down to make me great"* (Psalms 18:35). Here we have a very vivid Old Testament picture of the nature of grace. It beautifully illustrates the lengths to which God will go to bring us to Himself and to restore our worth as His sons and daughters. This verse reminds us that our lives are *valuable* because Jesus *stooped* and came down to our level so we could be reconciled to the Father and enjoy Him forever.

Yet, how many of us still believe that God accepts us on the basis of what we do for Him? We try to drag our tired carcasses out of bed early every morning to spend time with the Lord, we make attempts to witness to everything that breathes, and we sign up for as many projects as possible within our local congregations because we secretly believe that God is somewhat difficult to please. We think that His grace is only available to us after we've exhausted every other natural resource. We assume that we have to prove ourselves worthy of His love.

Our lives are *valuable* because Jesus *stooped* and came down to our level so we could be reconciled to the Father and enjoy Him forever.

Maybe this is why a lot of us are frustrated and burned out. We have replaced relationship with routine and delight with duty. We have tried to measure the success of our spiritual lives by living up to certain standards and expectations, but we have ended up feeling as if we can never do enough. We have focused so much on our "performance" that we have actually lost our "passion."

This is one of the primary reasons why approximately 50 percent of the pastors in America drop out of the ministry every year. Instead of living out of the loving acceptance and approval of their heavenly Father, they constantly strive to feel successful by the things they accomplish. Rather than finding their identity as Abba's child, they live as orphans, searching for significance in larger buildings, bigger budgets, and growing congregations. Some, out of their own insecurities, even *use* those who work for them merely to fulfill their own destinies. But how many of them end up spiritually and emotionally bankrupt because they become trapped in the destructive web of performance?

Several years ago, I was invited to speak at a leaders' retreat in Alabama. I was asked to teach the first session because the man who was in charge of the meetings wanted those who were there to be introduced to the message of *intimacy with God*. As I was speaking on the love of the Father, I noticed that not one of them was taking any notes and many of them were shuffling their feet and looking down at the ground.

Although I was somewhat surprised by what I was witnessing, it suddenly dawned on me that many of these pastors and leaders were uncomfortable with some of the things I was sharing. For one, I was reminding them that their core identity was not to be found in their ministries but in the fact that they were Abba's boys and girls. I also reiterated more than once that God had not called them to be "religious CEOs," but He wanted them to enjoy Him and to serve Him out of an understanding of His enjoyment of them. After the meeting was over, I realized that most of them were simply not used to the intimate language of the message of the Father's love and they were finding it hard to get in touch with their deepest feelings.

It was interesting to watch the reactions of these same leaders the next morning when the other speaker was introduced. He was a man who had planted several churches, and it was announced that he was going to be teaching on church growth. Almost everyone present was on the edge of their seats as he laid out a seven-point strategy for increasing the size of their churches and ministries. I was a bit shocked by what I was observing as many of them were vigorously taking notes.

At the end of the meeting the guest speaker was surrounded by a number of pastors who wanted to invite him to speak at their churches. This experience only confirmed to me that far too many Christian leaders have been programmed to believe they will only be considered successful when their churches or organizations reach a certain size. As much as I want to see authentic growth with disciples reproduced in our churches, we cannot be driven by the need to define our lives and ministries by our achievements.

Christian leaders must be more than successful fundraisers, administrative geniuses, captivating preachers, or brilliant scholars. True leaders are those who burn with an all-consuming passion for Christ. To them, power, prestige, and privilege are meaningless compared to knowing and loving Him.

Henri Nouwen once wrote:

> Christian leaders cannot simply be persons who have well-informed opinions about the burning issues of our time. Their leadership must be rooted in the permanent, intimate relationship with the incarnate Word, Jesus, and they need to find there the source for their words, advice, and guidance.... When we are securely rooted in personal

intimacy with the source of life, it will be possible to remain flexible but relativistic, convinced without being rigid, willing to confront without being offensive, gentle and forgiving without being soft, and true witnesses without being manipulative.[2]

All of us continually need to be reminded that God does not define our lives by what we do for Him. He defines our lives by who He created us to be for Himself. Somehow, each of us must dare to believe that our Father doesn't want our efforts nearly as much as He wants us. He is inviting us to celebrate His passion for us and all that He has provided through Jesus. He wants us to find our approval through the Cross rather than seeking to win His approval by what we do (see Eph. 1:6).

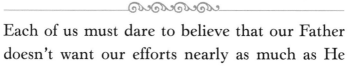

Each of us must dare to believe that our Father doesn't want our efforts nearly as much as He wants us.

This is primarily what Jesus was referring to when He said, "… *unless your righteousness exceeds the righteousness of the scribes and Pharisees, you will by no means enter the Kingdom of Heaven*" (Matt. 5:20 NKJV). Initially, when we read such a verse, we automatically assume that Christ is calling us to do more. But just the opposite is true. Having come to fulfill the Law (Torah), Jesus knew we couldn't measure up to its standards. The Law was given to remind men that they could never do enough to be accepted by God. To have a righteousness that exceeds the righteousness (self-effort) of the scribes and Pharisees means we must always acknowledge our spiritual bankruptcy apart from God's grace, actively resist every temptation to base our relationship with God on personal discipline, and aggressively embrace the righteousness of Christ as a free gift (see Matt. 5:3).

Because of the finished work of the Cross, you, as a believer, now have the same standing with the Father that Jesus has. No longer do you have to be afraid of not measuring up (see Rom. 8:15). The Christian life has never been about that. Christ's sacrifice and commitment to you guarantees that you are perfectly redeemed; therefore, you can lavishly obey and serve Him as a response of love. This is at the heart of what Jesus said in Matthew: *"You shall be perfect, just as your Father in Heaven is perfect"* (Matt. 5:48 NKJV). Obedience motivated by a fear of not measuring up or a fear of punishment is not the kind of obedience that pleases the Lord. Jesus deserves so much better and wants our obedience to be based on our affections for Him.

I am reminded of a quote that I saw in a day calendar—it was by Max Lucado taken from his book, *Come Thirsty*. He wrote, "With perfect knowledge of the past and perfect vision of the future, God loves you perfectly in spite of both. Perfect love can handle your fear of judgment."

THE FATHER'S LAVISH AFFECTIONS

A former student of mine sent me an e-mail last year describing some of the struggles she had gone through one morning during her quiet time with the Lord. She mentioned feeling like a *worm* because she believed she should be a better Christian after serving Him for a number of years. After having spent considerable time repenting for her lack of commitment and asking the Lord to change her, she sensed Him say to her, "Why do you see our times together as a means to an end? This is the end for Me. Our times together are what I died for."

The Father is extravagant in His affections for you. He continually longs for you. David expressed this beautifully in Psalms:

> *How precious also are Your thoughts to me, O God! How great is the sum of them! If I should count them, they would be more in number than the sand; when I awake, I am still with You* (Psalms 139:17-18 NKJV).

God is constantly thinking about you. You are always in His heart and on His mind. His thoughts about you outnumber the grains of sand on the seashores of the world. You are special to Him. There has never been or ever will be another person quite like you. You are not an accident. Abba uniquely made you for Himself, and you bring Him delight in a way no other human being can (see Ps. 139:13-14)! Father's lavish love for you is the crowning glory of your life on the earth!

As I state in my book, *Enjoying God*:

> "The truth is, God really likes you. In fact, He enjoys you. You may not think you measure up to supermodel or Mr. GQ status, but He does. Thanks to the gracious act of His Son, He sees you perfectly redeemed.
>
> He isn't tolerating you. He isn't putting up with you. He isn't waiting for you to get older or more mature in your Christian walk before He can love or enjoy you. He loves

you right where you are. Through the blood of Jesus, you're perfectly redeemed. That means that if you're a tennis player, then you've served an ace. If you're a baseball player, you've hit a home run. If you're a golfer, you've shot a hole in one. Do you get the point? This is what He sees. He's not keeping a record of your mistakes or the times you blew it. His blood takes care of those things. All He sees is you—and He enjoys you. Forever you will make Him ecstatic."[3]

ENDNOTES

1. Anthony DeMello, *The Way to Love* (New York, NY: Doubleday, 1991), 64.

2. Henry J.M. Nouwen, *In the Name of Jesus* (New York, NY: Crossroad, 1989), 42.

3. S.J. Hill, *Enjoying God* (Orlando, FL: Relevant Books, 2001), 3-4.

CHAPTER 5

Kingdom Contemplation

ED PIOREK

"We are put on earth for a little space that we might learn to bear the beams of love."

—William Blake

My contemplative journey began in the middle of a fearful night in 1967. As I was spiraling into despair following the tragic death of my mother, Jesus stepped into my bedroom and saved me. His presence brought a supernatural peace to my anxious heart. From that point on I had a deep desire to live in that presence. For the next 15 years, I nurtured my relationship with Jesus through a life of private devotion. As a conservative evangelical Christian, my contemplation focused on prayerful meditation on the Word of God. In my early Christian zeal I remember setting the alarm to wake up at two in the morning just to listen to my favorite Bible programs on the radio. I could feel the Lord's nearness in the darkness.

However, in the early 1980s after ten years in pastoral ministry, I found myself in a state of spiritual burnout, hungering for more of the presence of God in my life. At that time I had a providential meeting with John Wimber, the founder of the Vineyard churches. When John lay hands on me and prayed, I experienced a powerful infilling of the Spirit. I was introduced to the Person of the Spirit and the supernatural realm of spiritual gifts. God's heavenly Kingdom became a present reality in my life. This led to a new intimacy with the Spirit, anticipating His presence in my contemplative prayer times. I did less talking and more listening. I began hearing His voice and feeling His touch. His presence often moved me to tears.

Years later, I discovered that the tears were a result of feeling the love of God the Father. Up until that point I had not experienced the Father's love in a definable way. I knew that He loved me in the theological sense but not in a heartfelt way. I thought God was like my dad, and that if I failed to do things just right I would experience His rejection. The fear of failure began to plague my life and ministry. Then one wonderful day during a ministry time at a leaders' conference, the heavens opened and the Spirit fell on me. Then I heard a voice speak to me: "Eddie, you are My son and I love you. You can never fail in My sight." Tears flowed as the love of my heavenly Father filled my heart. As my insecurities were washed away, intimacy with Abba was born. The ongoing experience of His unconditional love is one of the greatest rewards of the secret life of contemplation.

According to the Oxford English Dictionary, contemplation is a form of prayer in which a person seeks a direct experience of the divine. Looking back on my contemplative journey, I see now that I have been in an ongoing discovery of what it means to have direct experience with the three Persons of the Godhead: Father, Son, and Spirit.

The Community of Love

In 1999 I was diagnosed with leukemia. During my year-long crisis with cancer, contemplation took on a new level of meaning. Up to that point, contemplation was a disciplined luxury. I did it because I wanted to enhance my relationship with God in the midst of a demanding schedule. Cancer caused contemplation to become an essential for survival. In the midst of chemotherapy treatment, the effects of the disease, the toxicity of the protocol, and extreme weight loss brought me to a point of nearly absolute weakness. My limit on a daily walk was about 50 yards. My eyesight faded as the day progressed, leaving me unable to read. I wasn't strong enough to help my wife lift dishes out of the dishwasher. All routine work in the ministry was discontinued. I was away from my office for more than six months. Miraculously, I preached every Sunday, sitting on a stool after being supported into the church. As a result of all this, my familiar touchstones for finding God's presence were gone. I spent most of my day at home and there I discovered new depths of blessing in contemplation.

On hot, summer days when I couldn't go outside, I would sit alone on our living room sofa and gaze on my beloved rose garden. I didn't have the energy to pray so I simply whispered "Jesus" again and again. After awhile I would feel a peaceful presence begin to wrap itself around me. I would just soak in the silence. No words were spoken. Sometimes I would cry a little as I felt a deep relief. These moments were transcendent. I felt as though I was somehow lifted up out of my suffering and held in a heavenly embrace. This experience was repeated afternoon after afternoon. It would also occur while I sat for hours receiving my chemotherapy injections. It would happen in the shower as I stretched out my arms to the walls to hold myself upright. With each short prayer, the presence of the Lord came again and again until the long battle was over. Praise the Lord, the cancer is gone, but the contemplation has remained.

I felt as though I was somehow lifted up out of my suffering and held in a heavenly embrace.

As I look back I realize that every time I cried out to Jesus, He drew near to me. As I hid myself in Him, the Spirit would come and surround me. As I clung to the Son, the Father would enfold me in His arms. I kept discovering that what lies at the very core of contemplation is a love relationship with the Trinity.

Many contemporary voices have taken up the theme of Trinitarian love. Experiencing this love is the focus of William Young's bestselling novel *The Shack*. In it we read of Mackenzie Phillips, a man facing tragedy, who finds healing in the loving presence of the Father, Son, and Holy Spirit. His encounter with God just so happens to take place in a very contemplative setting. Theological voices have also taken up this timely subject of the Trinity. As Christians we can be firm on our doctrinal understanding that there is one God who exists in three coequal, coeternal Persons—Father, Son, and Spirit—and yet we can forget that they live in a dynamic love relationship. Regent College's Darrel Johnson rehearses the perspective of the early church father Augustine:

> Augustine came to understand the three subsistences of the one essence in terms of love. The Father loves the Son, and the Son loves the Father. And according to Augustine, the bond of love between the Father and the Son is the Spirit.[1]

Dallas Willard puts it succinctly: "God in Himself is a sweet society of love."[2]

At the center of the universe is a community of love. We were created and redeemed to become part of that community. As my dear friend Jack Frost would enthusiastically say, "We are created for love!" Not only are we destined to live in that love forever in Heaven, but as disciples of Jesus we are meant to be fully immersed in that love now. Dallas Willard's paraphrase of the Great Commission found in Matthew 28:19 captures this prophetic sense of the deepening of Trinitarian experience:

> As you go throughout the world, make apprentices to Me from all kinds of people, *immerse them in Trinitarian reality,* and teach them to do everything I have commanded you.[3]

Every believer is to be immersed in the love flowing between the Father and Son by the Spirit. This image of baptism reminds me of when Jesus was baptized at the Jordan. As we look at that event we will gain a clearer picture of the dynamics of Trinitarian love and how contemplation has an important role in it.

A CONTEMPLATIVE EVENT

The Gospel of Mark describes the baptismal event in this way:

At that time Jesus came from Nazareth in Galilee and was baptized by John in the Jordan. As Jesus was coming up out of the water, He saw Heaven being torn open and the Spirit descending on Him like a dove. And a voice came from Heaven: "You are My son, whom I love; with You I am well pleased" (Mark 1:9-11).

Henri Nouwen, well-known author and Catholic priest, calls this baptism "one of the most central events"[4] in the life of Jesus. His baptism is central in the context of His experience of the Father's love while here on earth. To fully appreciate what Jesus experiences here, we need to remind ourselves of His humanity. Jesus is fully God and is also fully man. As a man He receives the anointing of the Spirit empowering Him for His public ministry and the affirmation of His Father's love (see Acts 10:38). Brennan Manning describes what Jesus must have experienced:

> I believe that at some point in His *human journey* Jesus was seized by the power of a great affection and experienced the love of His Father in a way that burst all previous boundaries of understanding.... Then it happens! Whatever the external manifestations were, the baptism of Jesus Christ in the River Jordan was an *awesome personal experience*. The heavens are split, the Spirit descends in the form of a dove, and Jesus hears the words, 'You are My Son, My Beloved, on You My favor rests.' What an *earthquake* in the human soul of Jesus![5]

If we step back and look at the baptismal event we get a glimpse of Trinitarian love. Remember Augustine's description: The Father loves the Son, the Son loves the Father, and the bond of love is the Spirit. We see the heavenly relationship of love manifest here on earth. As the Son stands in the baptismal waters, the Father declares His love for Him. The descending Spirit makes the bond of love an existential reality in the human heart of Jesus.

What is interesting is that Jesus entered this Trinitarian moment through contemplative prayer. In Luke we read that, "*...As He was praying, Heaven was opened and the Holy Spirit descended on Him...*" (Luke 3:21-22). Jesus, in touch with His human need, prays for the Spirit's anointing and the affirmation of His Father. He then moves into a passive, receptive posture in His prayer. He waits for a moment to let the Spirit rest on Him. He quiets himself to listen to His Father's tender voice of love. He receives the love being poured from Heaven into His heart. In this intimate moment, He presses into His Father's bosom (see John 1:18 NKJV). The heavenly Dove resting on the praying Christ portrays a beautiful image of contemplative prayer.

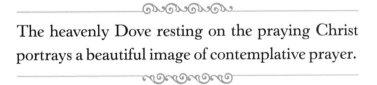

The heavenly Dove resting on the praying Christ portrays a beautiful image of contemplative prayer.

This contemplative aspect of Jesus' life continues through His years of ministry. He develops a rhythm of receptive prayer and active ministry. Often He goes to a place of solitude early in the morning to be alone with His Father. It is while in prayer on the Mount of Transfiguration and in the Garden of Gethsemane that Jesus enters into intimacy within the Trinitarian presence.

Jesus' baptism is prototypical for our Christian journey. It reveals the way into Trinitarian experience. We begin by standing in the waters of redemption through faith in Jesus. It continues by yielding to the Spirit's empowering presence. It is completed when we experience the love of our Father who has adopted us in Christ. Jesus' baptismal prayer provides a prototype for contemplative prayer. We come in our human weakness and pray in a restful and receptive manner. I have often called contemplative prayer "voluntary weakness" in that we are stepping away from the strengths of our own activity to receive and rest in the presence of God.

Here we learn the essential movement of contemplation. It begins with a focus on Jesus. We reverence the presence of Jesus in worship, prayer, and the reading of His Word. In doing so, we press into intimacy with Him much like the beloved disciple at the Last Supper. As we find ourselves in Christ, the Trinitarian reality unfolds around us.

The movement continues as the heavens open and the Spirit is poured out from Heaven into the depths of our hearts. The Kingdom presence from above makes the kingdom within our heart an existential reality. Dallas Willard affirms this heavenly source of the heart renovation found in contemplation: "The spiritual renovation and the 'spirituality' that comes from Jesus is nothing less than an invasion of natural human reality by a supernatural life 'from above.'"[6] This reality is birthed at conversion, empowered by infillings, and deepened through contemplation. As "kingdom contemplatives" we embrace both the Spirit's inbreaking from above and outworking from within.

Finally, we see that pressing into Jesus will lead us into the depths of the Father's heart of love. Fr. Thomas Keating describes the movement in this way:

> Christ leads us to the Father, but to the Father as He knows Him.... This is to follow Christ into the bosom of the Father where, as the Eternal Son, He surrenders to the divine source from whom He eternally emerges—and returns—in the love of the Holy Spirit. [7]

As we come into our Father's presence we can feel the warmth of His arms of love embracing us, gently pulling us to His breast. There we can hear His heartbeat and tender words of love. We become the beloved. Here our hearts are secured by the very source of love found only in God our Father.

Once we discover the joy of the contemplative experience, we will have a desire to incorporate it into our lives. Like Jesus, we can establish a rhythm of resting in prayer in the midst of a very busy life of work and ministry. There will be times when we go out to meet with God in the living room before the sun rises. Sometimes He will even call us to the mountain.

Several years ago, I felt called to visit a Benedictine monastery nestled in the mountains overlooking Santa Barbara, California. It was my first experience of the divine offices of prayer and periods of silence. I was made aware of the discipline of silence when my zealous "Good morning!" to a monk was met by a quiet smile and upturned eyebrow. As I went through the rhythm of praying, antiphonal singing, and taking quiet walks in the gardens I realized there were none of the normal stimulations for a powerful encounter with God. No worship band, charismatic preaching, or "Come Holy Spirit!" ministry times—only simplicity, silence, and empty space.

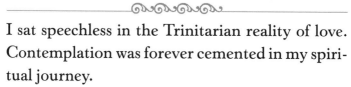

I sat speechless in the Trinitarian reality of love. Contemplation was forever cemented in my spiritual journey.

On my second day I attended the Eucharist. It would be a Lord's Supper I will never forget. Once again I sat in the silence in the rather austere chapel as the monks assembled. As we read Scriptures and sang a cappella, the bread and the cup were prepared. When the invitation was given I moved in line to receive the Sacraments. I prayerfully focused on coming into the presence of the Lord Jesus. As I savored the taste of the bread and the sweet wine I closed my eyes and prayed under my breath, "Lord Jesus have mercy on me." Immediately I was in His brilliant presence. I felt my body tremble as the Holy Spirit quietly yet powerfully flowed through me. I slowly walked to my seat and stood in the presence of the Lord. There, tears began to run down my cheek as Abba Father held me in His arms. I sat speechless in the Trinitarian reality of love. Contemplation was forever cemented in my spiritual journey.

CONTEMPLATIVE PRAYER

I first began to see the link between contemplative prayer and a deeper experience of the Father's love through the writing of Henri Nouwen, who was trained in the historic traditions of contemplation. In his writings, he describes the movement of contemplative prayer into a place of solitude and silence where we encounter the Father's love:

Solitude begins with a time and a place for God, and God alone.... It is precisely where we are most alone, most unique, most ourselves, that God is closest to us. That is where we experience God as our divine, loving Father...the real work of prayer is to become silent and listen to the voice that says good things about me...to discover there the small intimate voice saying: "You are My Beloved Child."[8]

Nouwen, Thomas Merton, and other writers helped me, as an evangelical Protestant, to learn from the contemplative experiences of Christians in the Catholic and Eastern Orthodox traditions. As I began to read about the lives of prominent contemplative people throughout church history, I saw that many had profound experiences of God's love and power. I discovered that St. Gregory the Great, at the end of the sixth century, described contemplation as "the knowledge of God that is impregnated with love."[9]

Perhaps the most articulate in describing the contemplative journey into God's love is the sixteenth-century Carmelite, St. John of the Cross. He has been acclaimed as one of the church's great mystics— indeed, a genius of mystical theology. His mystical theology describes the path by which "the soul is united in love with God." John was a contemporary of St. Teresa of Avila (1515–1582), working with her in Spain and pioneering spiritual innovation during the era of the notorious Spanish Inquisition. He was imprisoned and beaten for nine months. This period of forced solitude led to his well-known work, *The Dark Night of the Soul.* The intense purification of his soul led to a greater personal experience of the intimacies of Trinitarian love captured in another classic work *The Living Flame.* There he writes:

Since this soul is so close to God that it is transformed into a flame of love, in which the Father and the Son, and the Holy Spirit are communicated to it, what is so unbelievable about saying that it enjoys a foretaste of eternal life? ...The Blessed Trinity inhabits the soul by divinely illumining its intellect with the wisdom of the Son, delighting its will in the Holy Spirit, and by absorbing it powerfully and mightily in the delightful embrace of the Father's sweetness.[10]

PRACTICING CONTEMPLATIVE PRAYER

The classic movement of contemplative prayer looks something like this. It begins by going to a place of *solitude* where you can be alone with God. We, like Jesus, need to establish times and places for contemplation amidst our busy lives. Almost every morning I go off to the quiet of my bedroom just to be alone with the Lord. Many afternoons I take a break and go surfboarding in the waves off the California coast. I make the ocean my "board-room" and there prayerfully bask in Abba's presence.

Once we are alone the emphasis of contemplation is on *silence*. Our primary desire is simply to bring our hearts into a place of loving intimacy with God. The secret to contemplative prayer is speaking less and leaving more silent space for the Spirit to fill. In the quiet place we listen for the voice of love. Sometimes, as with young lovers, we experience the silence of love as our hearts are enveloped in the very presence the Trinity.

However, entering silence is not always easy. There is the problem of noise—both external and internal. Upon closing the door of the bedroom, an inner door opens with a flood of thoughts. Which brings us to the use of what many mystical writers call the *sacred word*. This word can be in the form of a short Scripture, a simple prayer, or even the sounds of soaking worship. These words help our ever-active minds to concentrate our intention on entering the presence of the Lord.

One useful historical practice is *lectio divina*—the slow, meditative reading of the Bible. When you meditate on a short Bible verse it brings you into the presence of the Word who authored it. The focus of meditation is to let the Word descend from our head into our heart and there encounter the presence of the Lord.

Another practice is praying short "arrow" or "breath" prayers such as the famous Jesus Prayer, "Lord Jesus, have mercy on me." Praying the Jesus Prayer reverently and repetitively, taking breaths of the Spirit in between, quickly centers me in the Lord's presence. My wife favors the one line, "Give us this day our daily bread," from the Our Father or Lord's Prayer. The bread of His presence always comes to feed her soul.

Sometimes we can sense the Spirit surrounding us, breaking in from Heaven above. Other times it seems like gentle waters rising out of His indwelling presence.

In between the words we must leave breathing room for the *Spirit's presence*. Sometimes we can sense the Spirit surrounding us, breaking in from Heaven above. Other times it seems like gentle waters rising out of His indwelling presence. These descriptions are often based on theological, mystical, or personal paradigms. In any case it is the manifest presence of the Spirit engaging us, making our contemplation a Kingdom reality, bringing us into intimacy of relationship with the Father and the Son.

As we linger in contemplation we will find ourselves slowly being *saturated in love* as we become immersed in the Trinitarian presence. We are drawn into the great love affair of the Trinity. We can experience Jesus loving us. We enter into the intimacy of loving Him. We can experience the Father's love for us. Whenever I feel the touch of the Spirit I remember that He is the bond of love making the Father's embrace real to me.

Sometimes the love is manifest in gentle quieting of our souls. At other times the floodgates open wide and our hearts are flooded with a pure Trinitarian love beyond description.

As a result of my battle with cancer, I went through a challenging time in ministry. We had decided to merge our congregation with another Vineyard Church. At that time, my wife Janet and I met with another couple who were close friends for a casual meal. Over dinner they told us that they wouldn't be continuing with us in the new church configuration. They would be leaving us the next Sunday. It was a bit shocking. I passed on dessert.

When I got up the next morning I felt a deep sadness over the loss. I went into my bedroom and knelt down to pray. In the silence I sighed and began to pray slowly and repeatedly, "Lord Jesus, have mercy on me." After awhile I felt the Spirit's presence resting on me. I lifted my hands up and welcomed Him. Then I heard these words impressed strongly on my mind, "Don't you know that I will never leave you?" Whether those words were from the Father or the Son, I don't know, but I know that my grieving heart was immediately pierced by love. I wept as a river of deep reassurance flowed through me. As I rose up I was at peace again with a new strength to move forward.

RESTING IN THE RIVER OF LOVE

One of the most popular biblical metaphors for God's presence flowing from Heaven to earth is that of the river (see Rev. 22:1-2; Ezek. 47). The river of God describes the Spirit's movement into our contemplation, church gatherings, conferences, and out into the world. To many involved in renewal, this river is a tangible reality. We can enter into it and go for a swim! When we do we discover that the river is not an impersonal force but actually the manifestation of the Trinitarian presence. We meet the Father, Son, and Spirit there in an outpouring of perfect love. Fr. Thomas Keating again:

> The Trinitarian relationships, of their very nature, invite us into the stream of divine love that is unconditional and totally self-surrendered. This boundless love emerges from the Father into the Son, and through the Son is communicated to all creation. The invitation is given to every human being to enter the stream of divine love, or at least to venture a big toe into the river of eternal life.[11]

RESTING IN LOVE

We can enjoy this inner river by simply resting in contemplative prayer. It is as if we just lie back and float in this eternal river and let it carry our soul forward in the purposes of the Kingdom. One of the greatest benefits of entering into the river of love is the profound experience of rest we find there. In the flow of the

Father's perfect love, we are free from expending energy to try to earn it, and that is a big relief. This eternal river also fills us with its energizing power, and that's a great boost to our lives.

> One of the greatest benefits of entering into the river of love is the profound experience of rest we find there.

John and Carol Arnott are two friends of mine who have discovered the secret of resting in the river of love in the midst of an incredibly demanding schedule. John and Carol pastor the Toronto Airport Christian Fellowship in Ontario, Canada. They have been giving leadership to a remarkable outpouring of the Spirit, popularly known as the Toronto Blessing, which began in January 1994. Nearly 4 million people have visited the church over the last ten years, and the outpouring has spread all over the world. John and Carol have been ministering almost nonstop all that time.

In traveling with them, I have been amazed at their boundless energy in preaching and praying for countless people during long hours of ministry. What impresses me most is how relaxed they are in the midst of it. They seem to be at ease and not in a rush to get things done. When they minister they care for each person with sensitivity, compassion, and Kingdom authority. I have never heard them raise their voices to make something happen or panic when nothing has. I wondered how they managed to stay in such a loving flow throughout the years.

During a conference in Dresden in 2002, I caught a glimpse of how they stay in such a good place. After a lunch break we were talking about how faithful the Father was in bringing us into the central event of His love in Germany. As we stood to return to the next session, John and Carol took my hands and we formed a circle to pray to thank the Father for what He had been doing. Many people had been saved, healed, and filled with the Father's love. As the Spirit gently overwhelmed us, all three of us found ourselves lying on our backs on the floor. No one got up. We were just floating on our backs in the river of God's love. After awhile, John reached his hand over, put it on my knee, and said, "Eddie, it doesn't get any better than this." Amazing! Here I was lying on the cafeteria floor with John and Carol Arnott, experiencing their secret to success in ministry.

They took time in the middle of their busy conference schedule just to love God and let Him love them back. What mystics called contemplation they call "soaking in the Spirit." They tell me that they now begin almost every day this way. Putting on some worship music, they lie down on the floor and just soak in this river of love. It is not hard to see the source of their loving ministry.

KINGDOM ACTION

Kingdom contemplation leads to Kingdom action. Time spent in the private presence of God will always lead to the public extension of His Kingdom. As with Jesus at His baptism our contemplative experience of the Father's love will simultaneously commission us to show His compassion to others. In her classic *The Interior Castle*, Teresa of Avila describes the movement from resting to doing good works:

> For if the soul is much with Him, as it is right it should
> be, it will seldom think of itself: its whole thought will

be concentrated upon finding ways to please Him and upon showing Him how much it loves Him. This, my daughters, is the aim of prayer...of which are born good works and good works alone.[12]

Some of the early saints of the church demonstrated that their times in solitude led to encounters with God that catalyzed remarkable ministry when they returned to public life. Saint Antony of Egypt (251–356) was called to twenty years of isolation in the desert where he sought God, fought demons, and was rescued by an incredible visitation of Jesus. Henri Nouwen describes the results of his contemplative journey:

When he emerged from his solitude, people recognized in him the qualities of an authentic 'healthy' man, whole in body, mind and soul. They flocked to him for healing, comfort and direction.[13]

St. Antony had a significant ministry of signs and wonders following his hidden years. This was typical of other contemplatives. St. Catherine of Siena (1347–1380) spent three years enclosed in her room. Robert Ellsburg describes the results:

The next several years found her nursing the sick, distributing alms to the poor, and ministering to prisoners and plague victims. Through miraculous healings and her air of spiritual authority, she began to attract disciples.[14]

In 2005 I was privileged to speak at Toronto Airport's Soaking in God's Glory Conference with Heidi Baker. During my morning session I taught on contemplative prayer and then led everyone in praying the Jesus Prayer. Even though the Spirit powerfully visited us I was a bit unsure about the topic being a renewal focus. I was greatly reassured when Heidi came up to me after and said that Henri Nouwen was one of her favorite authors and that her doctoral dissertation had been on the Desert Fathers. Later she gave me a beautiful card with a picture of her and some of her adopted children from Mozambique. Inside it is written this prayer: "Lord Jesus Christ, Beautiful Savior, have mercy on me, Your beloved." She then added, "I pray this for several hours every day."

During that 2005 conference, my eyes were opened to the paradox that resting in the river of the Trinitarian presence will lead to our rising up in the power of the Kingdom. We spent many hours in "soaking worship." At times I felt waves of love flowing through me bringing tears, laughter, and deep peace. There were transcendent moments of what I could only describe as "pure love."

I could only imagine the healing power we might see if we fully entered into the synergy of love within the Trinity.

Then there were memorable ministry times. I went to pray for a man who came forward for healing prayer. He was in pain from a severe injury to his back and could not bend over. I have to admit that I didn't see myself with a great healing gift. My prayer for him wasn't filled with faith. My interview after seemed to confirm that as not much had changed. While we talked I looked at my right hand and it was glistening with oil! I was so amazed I showed it to the injured man and said, "Look at that! Let's pray again!" Putting my hand on his back, the power of the Spirit touched him and he was immediately healed! I saw soaking lead to signs and wonders! I could only imagine the healing power we might see if we fully entered into the synergy of love within the Trinity.

We live in a time when the Kingdom of God is expanding throughout the world at an exponential rate. The gospel of Jesus Christ is being preached with signs and wonders following. The Spirit is being poured out in power upon all flesh. The love of the Father is being revealed to a fatherless generation. Simultaneously, there is a growing interest in contemplative prayer. The spirituality of the Desert Fathers and monastic saints is being rediscovered in all the various spheres of the modern church. Contemplative prayer, long embraced by liturgical churches, has had a reawakening through people like Henri Nouwen and Thomas Keating. Evangelical Christians are embracing it with the term "spiritual direction." Those with charismatic and Pentecostal leanings may call it "soaking."

I believe we are part of a great contemplative prayer movement. It is a movement that both reaches back to appreciate its roots in early Church history and reaches forward to apprehend the end-time move of God. As the Kingdom comes, the Kingdom contemplative will be there to welcome it.

ENDNOTES

1. Darrel Johnson, *Experiencing the Trinity* (Vancouver: Regent College, 2002), 50.

2. Dallas Willard, *Renovation of the Heart* (Colorado Springs, CO: NavPress, 2002), 184.

3. Ibid., 240.

4. Henri Nouwen, *Here and Now: Living in the Spirit* (New York, NY: Crossroad, 1994), 99.

5. Brennan Manning, *The Signature of Jesus* (Sisters, OR: Multnomah, 1996), 166-167.

6. Willard, 19.

7. Thomas Keating, *Intimacy with God* (New York, NY: Crossroad, 1994), 37.

8. Henri Nouwen, *The Only Necessary Thing: Living a Prayerful Life* (New York, NY: Crossroad, 1999), 42-43, 150.

9. Keating, 39.

10. Kieran Kavanaugh, ed., *John of the Cross: Selected Writings* (New York, NY: Paulist Press, 1987), 296, 298-99.

11. Keating, 150.

12. St. Teresa of Avila, *Interior Castle* (New York, NY: Doubleday, 1989), 228.

13. Henri Nouwen, *The Way of the Heart: Desert Spirituality and Contemporary Ministry* (San Francisco, CA: HarperCollins, 1991), 19-20.

14. Ibid., 19-20.

CHAPTER 6

Friendship With Jesus: The Way to Intimacy With God

DR. STEPHAN VOSLOO

Genuine acceptance removes fear and hiding, and creates freedom to know and be known. In this freedom arises a fellowship and sharing so honest and open and real that the persons involved dwell in one another. There is union without loss of individual identity. When one weeps, the other tastes salt. It is only in the Triune relationship of Father, Son and Spirit that personal relationship of this order exists, and the early Church used the word 'perichoresis' to describe it. The good news is that Jesus Christ has drawn us within this relationship and its fullness and life are to be played out in each of us and in all creation.

—C. Baxter Kruger[1]

Two of my children were good friends with their spouses for a couple of years before they found out that they were actually in love. During this time they learned how to communicate, enjoy things together, and resolve conflict before they realized that there was more involved than just hanging out together. For a long time the truth was crystal clear to everyone around them, but they kept on denying it, and we eventually decided to let sleeping dogs lie. And then it just happened. Love was stirred and their best friends became the center of their young lives. Somewhere a connection was made. The next level of intimacy was ordained, but they needed to build a relationship before they could enter into it.

Don't we all seek intimacy? Some will never acknowledge it, and for some the desire has been so deeply buried that they can't even recognize it. We all seek a place of safety where we know we will not be rejected. We all seek a place of interaction where we can feel another human being—intellectually, spiritually, physically. Deep down in our core we need to be loved and to love because we were made in the image of a God who is love. Subconsciously, and at times consciously, we crave to give this love away and to receive it from both humans and from God. It is probably the most original desire we are capable of.

If we look at the marriages around us then it seems that friendship remains the best preparation for intimacy. Those who built their marriages on the hormonal response to physical intimacy before they learned how to be friends just seem to be worse off. Is it possible that the same could be true about our relationship with God?

Some relationships are so shallow that there is scarcely any communication except for the absolute essentials. Many people who call themselves Christians talk to God only for a couple of minutes a day, unless they are in trouble, of course, or fighting with Him. As in the case of marriages, these people miss out on the real reason for being together with God or a spouse. We can develop a relationship that is so intimate that it provides the perfect medium for real unconditional love to flow and for our most basic desire to be fulfilled. It is possible to experience now, on a physical level, some of what God has ordained for us for eternity. Friendship is the bridge over the divide between singleness and intimacy. It works best in human relationships and it has been overlooked in the quest for relationship with God.

TAKING SHORT CUTS DOESN'T WORK

In our human relationships, we often replace the longer process of developing friendship with either effort or emotional fervor. Some want to work their way into intimacy, and others want their emotions to lead them there. Neither discovers the real essence of love. For to discover real love, you need to get to know the person. We tend to do the same with God. We want to work for Him and so get to know Him, or we want to be swept off our feet by emotion and end up in His arms.

Real love requires a sense of unconditional acceptance. It is difficult to find it from a hard taskmaster or from a one-night stand. We may find emotional gratification in the physical unity, but it is only for a fleeting moment or for a season. Intimacy with God is never a reward for hard work. We will always be disappointed with His reaction to our efforts. He is just not moved at all by effort, because the love response He seeks from us is a response to incredible grace. The intimacy of real, unconditional acceptance is given freely. Most of our Christian journey is about discovering that love.

THE STORY OF AMAZING LOVE

Jesus told the parable of the prodigal son to teach about the love of the Father. Both the sons struggled because they had no idea how much the father loved them. Both their journeys were supposed to lead to one end—to know the kind of love that can allow a son to take his inheritance prematurely, then wait for him to squander everything and run to embrace him in a feast of forgiveness when he returns. The prodigal accepted that love and experienced its glory. The older brother was so stuck in his offense that he could not recognize the spectacle of love that was playing itself out right in front of his eyes. He refused to enter into the feast of grace and acceptance and remained outside groveling in his self pity. Was that very different than the pigsty his younger brother had to leave?

The feast is the place of intimacy where we learn the secret of the love of the Father. The love is hidden until it is manifested in the unconditional acceptance of an unlovable prodigal, and if I am not the prodigal I can barely understand it. The woman who broke the alabaster jar on the feet of Jesus understood this love. The Pharisees who looked on could not. She enjoyed the promises of intimacy, but they were bound in their offence. She was commended by Jesus while they were called a "brood of vipers."

We have to walk away from our achievements and find the nothingness of humility before we can understand this love of the Father.

Just as the building of a friendship requires that we vacate our selfish positions and find the common ground of humility where the friendship is more important than self, we have to walk away from our achievements and find the nothingness of humility before we can understand this love of the Father. There is a journey to travel before we get there. The elder brother refused to travel that journey away from self and never discovered the love. Humility is the foundation of friendship, and pride the one force that destroys it. Pride causes us to hold on to our rights and expectations. Pride apportions responsibilities to the other party without taking any for itself. It establishes laws and expects performance. Friendship creates the ideal atmosphere where we can let go of our pride and embrace the humility of gentleness, being willing to yield to the demands of the relationship for the sake of finding the security of true intimacy.

Emotions and effort create the exact opposite environment. They speak the language of achievement, comparison, and competition and fail to achieve the reality of intimacy because they find fulfillment in the pride of success and emotional achievement. We can let go of all that in the safety of hanging out with a real friend.

Life taught the prodigal a lesson in humility that prepared him to receive the love of the father and enter into the feast. The older brother was too busy working for his inheritance and too proud of his achievements to receive unconditional love. Love precedes inheritance.

LOVING AN UNSEEN FATHER

The father Jesus portrayed in this parable is the Father who is yearning to have a relationship with us. He has an inheritance for us born from love. He called us His children and bestowed on us the inheritance of intimacy on the basis of our DNA. He wants to give us our inheritance, not let us work for it. He loves us while we use it for our own gain, He waits for our return from the faraway land of effort and striving, and He runs to meet us while we are still reciting our lame excuses.

This loving Father knew how difficult it would be for us to relate to a Spirit Being who is both unseen and far removed from our highest thoughts. He did not want us to conjure up images of Him to relate to, because He knew that we would create our own idols and serve our own images. So He sent us a picture of Himself. He came in the form of a Man to establish for us a beachhead into relationship with the unseen, into intimacy with the Creator. God revealed Himself in the form of Jesus so that we can have Someone to relate to and find a Friend who could lead us across the divide and introduce us to the unseen Father.

Many find it difficult to build a friendship with the Father. We tend to relate to Him as we relate to our earthly fathers. Although most of us may know that they love us, we expect them to give us instructions, to train us through example, rebuke, and discipline. Most of us are ready to obey our fathers and to work for them. Most people—especially the men—expect words of affection and love from their mothers but not from their fathers. We expect praise for effort and encouragement when we achieve but not "sappy" words of love. Dad is often removed, the traditional patriarch who encourages sons to work and do their best, not the one who is our friend. That is obviously not the universal experience but certainly the most common one.

Therefore, Father had to manifest Himself in another form and had to first call us into another relationship. Here, we would be free to be ourselves—without performance and desire for recognition and praise—as preparation for real intimacy. Only when we are ourselves can we be good friends. He gave us friendship with His Son to prepare us to receive the love He desires to pour out on us.

THE ESSENCE OF FRIENDSHIP

St. Augustine said, "A friend is someone who knows everything about you and still accepts you."[2] Brennan Manning paints a fuller picture:

> A friend is someone who stays with you in the bad weather of life, guards you when you are off your guard, restrains your impetuosity, delights in your presence, forgives your failures, does not forsake you when others let you down, and shares whatever he or she might be having for breakfast (as Jesus did on the beach along the Sea of Tiberius)—fish and chips, moon pie, cold pizza or chocolate cake and milk.[3]

This was Father's plan. He sent us a Friend who can share our lives because He knows our struggles and pain. He sent us a Friend to experience life with us—the everyday, get-up-for-work life—the disappointments of real life, the highs of achievement, the lows of failure, the joys of love, and the pain of separation. He came to set a table in the face of our enemies when we are losing the good fight in the valley of shadows and tasting the bitterness of failure.

The Son had to come in our form and be our Friend so that He can show us what the highest expression of love is—to lay down your life for your friend. We would never have been able to know the beauty of friendship that sustains to the ultimate without having seen this picture.

He used the metaphor of friendship because He wants us to discern the difference between working for a boss and just hanging out with a buddy.

Jesus killed the notion that we are called to "serve" Him. According to John, He specifically said that He does not call us servants anymore, but He calls us friends. Jesus said:

> *I'm no longer calling you servants because servants don't understand what their master is thinking and planning. No, I've named you friends because I've let you in on everything I've heard from the Father* (John 15:15 MSG).

His position did not change. Father is still the master, but our position has changed. We are now allowed into the mysteries of the discussion between Father, Son, and Holy Spirit. By laying down His life, our Friend invited us into the inner circle, and we can know as much as He does. And that has changed our status. We are not serving anymore, we are participating!

By laying down His life, our Friend invited us into the inner circle, and we can know as much as He does. We are not serving anymore, we are participating!

According to Jesus, the condition of entering into this privilege is friendship, not anointing or martyrdom or perfection. So friendship becomes very important; maybe it becomes more important than obedience.

This is the question we have to find an answer to—what comes first, obedience or friendship? Does Jesus call us friends because we obey the law, or does He just call us friends and hang out with us in a relationship so rich that it is able to change our lives, and then we naturally do what He wants us to do? He will never demand anything from our flesh, for He knows that *"in me (that is, in my flesh) nothing good dwells"* (Rom. 7:18 NKJV). It is only us who do not know that and who are trying to rehabilitate fleshly behavior patterns. He comes and lives in us, and as we allow His life to be lived through us, we can achieve even the command, *"Therefore you shall be perfect, just as your Father in Heaven is perfect"* (Matt. 5:48 NKJV). Only His life can fully obey the law, so obedience can never precede redemption, and redemption brings us into friendship.

Because Jesus said, *"You are My friends if you do whatever I command you,"* religion demands obedience as a condition for friendship (John 15:14 NKJV). But, in the same breath, He said, *"Greater love has no one than this, than to lay down one's life for his friends"* (John 15:13 NKJV). And then He lay down His life for us, signifying that we were friends already. Not friends because we have been obedient. If obedience could open the way to friendship, then I did not need the Cross. The Cross brought the potential for friendship, and as His friend I became the fourth member of the eternal discourse.

Participating in the Divine Discourse

Friendship with Jesus is the first step across the divide into the thoughts of the Father. We need a guide for this journey and the guide has to be both man and God. We need a Man who knows the pain and whom we can trust, and we need God to interpret for us the mysteries of the Divine discourse. That is why Jesus is the Way, the Truth, and the Life. He is the way to the Father. He knows the truth about our human condition, and He gives the life that sustains us on the journey. He is the Father's gift to us, for only Father knew that intimacy with the unseen God requires more than just forgiveness or obedience or perfection. The divide is too wide; we will never make it to Him without the support of a Friend.

Jesus is not asking us to keep laws. He asks us to love. But friendship precedes intimacy. Has Father given us this Friend to teach us how to love Him? Can this be the deeper meaning behind what Paul said to the Corinthians? *"Now all things are of God, who has reconciled us to Himself through Jesus Christ...that is, that God was in Christ reconciling the world to Himself..."* (2 Cor. 5:18-19 NKJV). The reconciliation starts with redemption but continues through the guidance of a Friend who *is* the Way and *knows* the way to the heart of a Father who is waiting for the return of both His prodigal *and* His dutiful Son.

I am convinced that friendship with Jesus is not a nice-to-have; it is no add-on or something we can afford to desire from a distance. It is an essential requirement if we really want to penetrate the depths of intimacy with the Father.

FOCUSING IN THE RIGHT PLACE

If that is true and we do desire intimacy with Father, then where should our focus be? Should we focus on spiritual exercises, practicing the disciplines of the spiritual life, worship, intercession, or keeping religious sacraments? Maybe we should focus on building a relationship with our Friend, on hanging out with Jesus the Man, who is our guide into the glory of the spiritual disciplines, the agony of intercession, and the sacrifice of true worship.

Friendship is not one-sided. It needs commitment, time, prioritizing, and above all, the sharing of life together. The more experiences we share together and the more memories we make as we face the hardships and the joys of life together, the closer we become. We don't build friendships around boardroom tables or in the pews of our Sunday gatherings. We don't build friendships around physical relationships where the focus is on satisfying needs. We build friendships in the trenches of ordinary life.

The more experiences we share together and the more memories we make as we face the hardships and the joys of life together, the closer we become.

My best friends are those who have been with me through thick and thin, who know that I have failed them but are still there for me. We build friendships around coffee tables and dinner tables. We build friendship through sharing, talking, opening up, and giving of ourselves. Friendship without communicating is as improbable as baking bread without flour. We need to reveal our inner thoughts, fears, and hopes. We need to give and ask for unconditional acceptance. We need to talk.

Building friendship with Jesus is no different. He chose the metaphor after having experienced the joys and pain of friendships for 32 years.

And He used it to give us a clue to finding intimacy. While on earth, He modeled perfect friendship in the way He walked with His disciples, shared life with them, ate with them, spoke to them, cried with them, and rebuked them. The gospels are the evidence of the memories they made together, and the best of the Christian faith is the monument to the lasting power of that friendship. Then He sealed the example by doing exactly what He required of them. He laid down His life for His friends to show the ultimate expression of love. *"Greater love has no one than this, than to lay down one's life for his friends"* (John 15:13 NKJV). His willingness to die for sinners is the ultimate statement of unconditional acceptance and the final resting place for those who accept it. It is the rest of intimacy that we seek, it is unconditional acceptance that brings it about, and it is available on invitation.

The Invitation

This is the life He invites us into when He says:

> *Come to Me, all you who labor and are heavy laden, and I will give you rest. Take My yoke upon you and learn from Me, for I am gentle and lowly in heart, and you will find rest for your souls* (Matthew 11:28-29 NKJV).

The theme of humility runs thick in this invitation. Of all the things we could expect Him to teach us, this is what He knows we have to learn from Him—meekness and humility. Pride caused the separation, humility is the remedy. Without humility, we don't share our lives with one another. We don't communicate our deepest feelings, and we cut others out of our daily experiences and our inner lives. All He is asking is that we will come to Him, not to His doctrine or His miracles or His church or His provision. And we need to be humble to come without our achievements and without trying to achieve spiritual greatness. Because the end of this dispensation is a marriage feast, not a medal parade, we have to learn how to just hang out with Jesus instead of trying to impress Him with our spirituality.

He proved that He is interested in our lives and that He wants to share it with us by coming in our form. We need to allow Him to share in the mundane and sensational events that make our day. We have to learn how to talk to Him.

No other religion claims that its god lives inside the worshipers. That is what makes us unique. It is such a disaster when we do not grasp its potential. If we walk with Jesus all day we will be less inclined to break the law. If we repent from excluding Him by our silence we may have to repent less from sin. Inviting Jesus to sit on the couch and enjoy the movie we want to watch may have an immense effect on our choice of movie.

When we ask Jesus' advice about the spreadsheet we are working on or the cake we are baking, we will learn how ready He is to give his opinion. He is speaking all the time; it is us who are not recognizing His voice. The Creator of the universe has something to say about most things in His creation, and He is willing to voice that opinion to His friends. Many of the thoughts we have or the ideas we get come because He shares His wisdom freely, but because of our own silence, we do not expect an opinion and miss the blessing of giving Him glory.

THE JOURNEY

This is not a journey that we can travel alone or by our own effort. We have to be lead by our Friend. We will find out that we cannot make it happen—we are totally dependent on His grace. Brother Lawrence of the Resurrection was a sixteenth-century monk who lived a simple but profound life in the presence of God. He found a way to transcend the busyness of the monastery kitchen and his cobbler's shop. He looked for the presence of his Friend in every circumstance, asked help in everything, and thanked Him in constant conversation. He experienced a blessing of intimacy that went far beyond the regulated times of worship and devotion. His life was such an inspiration that it was described by his friend in a little Christian classic that has stood the test of time called *The Practice of the Presence of God*.

Br. Lawrence said:

> God alone is capable of making Himself known as He really is; we search in reasoning and in the sciences, as in a poor copy, for what we neglect to see in the original. God Himself paints Himself in the depths of our souls. We must enliven our faith and elevate ourselves by means of that faith above all our feelings, to adore God, the Father and Jesus Christ in their divine perfections. This way of faith is the mind of the church, and it suffices to arrive at high perfection.[4]

As we grow in humility, we grow in being content to ask and to wait. We stop demanding, and we rejoice in His kindness as He lavishes the gifts of His friendship on us. He does not give gifts when we achieve, as did our earthly fathers. We don't have to wait for a birthday or Christmas; He wants to show forth the riches of the glory of His grace in His kindness to us, and He enjoys giving us more of Himself at all times and in all situations (see Eph. 2:7). If He has given His life for us, why would He keep away from us the one revelation that has the potential to change us?

He wants to show forth the riches of the glory of His grace in His kindness to us, and He enjoys giving us more of Himself at all times and in all situations.

The more we see Jesus, the more fervent our prayer for more revelation becomes, because He consumes us with His love and draws us with cords of love and friendship. We still wander off into the faraway land of effort where the pleasures of both good and evil lure us to spend our inheritance, but there is no denying it anymore—we can become hooked on Jesus, and every day can be a day of discovering more of Him. Every discovery is more breathtaking than the one before, and every day we can fall deeper in love.

Br. Lawrence had a peculiar insight into this mystery that came from a lifetime of experiencing the immediacy of God. He said:

> The most intimate union with God is the actual presence of God. Although this relationship with God is totally spiritual, it is quite dynamic, because the soul is not asleep; rather, it is powerfully excited. In this state the soul is livelier than fire and brighter than the unclouded sun, yet, at the same time is tender and devout. This union is not a simple expression of the heart, like saying, 'Lord,

I love You with all my heart,' or similar words. Rather, it is an inexpressible state of the soul—gentle, respectful, humble, loving and very simple—that urges the person to love God, to adore Him and to embrace Him with both tenderness and joy.[5]

THE SEARCH

I think this is why Jesus told the parable of the merchant and the pearl of great price. The merchant had to see the pearl, touch it, and make sure that it was as precious as he had been told before he sold all to buy it. Somehow, man needed to see God to fall in love with Him, and in His mercy He sent us a Man to represent Him perfectly so that men and women could touch Him, hear Him teach, see Him love, lay on His breast, receive bread from His hand, see His blood flow down a Cross, and put their fingers in the scars on His wrists. They touched the Pearl. He has nothing less for us who believe in Him through what they taught us. The possibility of this kind of revelation is there; we are the poorer for not asking, yes, even begging for it.

Paul writes, *"But **of Him** you are in Christ Jesus"* (1 Cor. 1:30 NKJV). We have been given the Pearl; it is not far away from us. We don't have to ascend into Heaven to find it—it is near us, in our hearts and in our mouths (see Rom. 10:8). We have to ask, cry out with vehement cries and tears as Jesus did to Him who can save us from the death of never discovering this glorious friendship (see Heb. 5:7). And we will be heard, for it is His good pleasure to give us the Kingdom (see Luke 12:32).

Beyond Asking

On our journey of discovery, we should use our imagination—we have all been given the most glorious tool to facilitate dreams and bring hope. We should use it to seek the Treasure. We can place ourselves in imaginary situations while we wait in line or in traffic or during our intimate time with Him, and we can see Him with us having a cup of tea, walking next to us, sitting in the green pastures or beside the still waters—the way David did while he was caring for the sheep. Many of his psalms were the products of these flights of his imagination. We don't have to use what we hear and see to formulate doctrine or teach others or make a name for ourselves. We are perfectly safe if we keep our conversations a secret between friends and just use them for our own encouragement. These are times of intimate love and not times of instruction or briefing for a mission. We have more than enough of those—we need to hear Him say, "I love you...actually, I'm wild for you." Let it permeate our being and just wait to hear it again.

We sometimes need to tear ourselves away from our idols and look with our imaginative eye to see what Jesus is doing or give Him a loving look or be with Him for a moment. We need to encourage each other to know by faith that He will be there if we turn to Him. Oswald Chambers exhorts us to use our mind to place ourselves before Jesus:

> If you have never used your mind to place yourself before God, begin to do it now. There is no reason to wait for God to come to you. You must turn your thoughts and your eyes away from the face of idols and look to Him and be saved.

Your mind is the greatest gift God has given you and it ought to be devoted entirely to Him. You should seek to bring every thought into captivity to the obedience of Christ...(see 2 Cor. 10:5). Encourage yourself to remember, and your affections for God will increase tenfold.[6]

Frank Laubach decided to play his "game of minutes" to help him to turn to Jesus every minute of the day. He simply found things in his ordinary, very busy day to remind him to turn to Jesus in humility and ask for help, declare his love in simple sentences, or just be aware of His presence. He did what Br. Lawrence did—he practiced the presence of God in the mundane things. Like Br. Lawrence, his goal was to do all he did for the love of God. He was astounded by the results. See what he wrote in his diary on January 29, 1930:

I feel simply carried along each hour, doing my part in a plan which is far beyond myself. This sense of co-operation with God in little things is what astonishes me. I seem to have to make sure of only one thing now, and every other thing 'takes care of itself,' or I prefer to say what is more true, God takes care of all the rest. *My part is to live in this hour in continuous inner conversation with God and in perfect responsiveness to His will.* To make this hour gloriously rich. This seems to be all I need to think about.[7]

My part is to live in continuous inner conversation with my Friend and become totally responsive to His will. I have to talk to Him, look for His hand, touch the scars, feel His tears, and be a conduit for His life and love to flow. Nothing more. That is all I have to do—He will do the rest. We may have to develop habits that will facilitate this turning, especially in the beginning. As we grow in faith and confidence that He really wants this friendship more than we do, it becomes easier. As we grow in faith it becomes a natural way of life—a continuous state of being with Jesus.

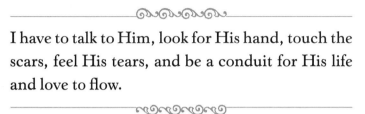

I have to talk to Him, look for His hand, touch the scars, feel His tears, and be a conduit for His life and love to flow.

THE CANVAS OF INTIMACY

The canvas of intimacy is eternity; the picture the Holy Spirit is painting for us is that of a dance that started before time and will continue beyond time. The participants in the dance are three Persons whose very essence is a love so great that they act as one. They love so much that the dividing lines become blurred in a movement so smooth and flowing that each Person has lost His identity in the other. One God, whose dance of love spilled over as a fountain of creative energy, to manifest their togetherness in creation.

William Long's illustration of the Argentine tango brought the canvas to life for me:

> Let me illustrate what I mean from Argentine tango (I take lessons every Monday night). My instructors tell me that tango is a dance in which the woman ought to be able to tell in the first thirty seconds whether the

man (her partner) would make a good husband. Why? Because there is something in the attentiveness of the man to his partner, the communication that takes place through gentle touching, the engagement through being 'centered' or 'square' with each other, that communicates to the other person that he is capable of and interested in being content with her alone. He isn't interested in showing off for the crowd or in twisting and turning in his own world. Love and fidelity, then, are believed to be communicated in the first thirty seconds.[8]

The picture illustrates a level of communication that requires total attention and complete dependence. This kind of dance requires an interdependence that can only be a product of the nothingness of true humility and the creativity of true desire. Not desire for gratification of self, but desire for the completion of a new whole, for the beauty of selflessness that creates a new person and, through the new unity, a perfect expression of creative movement. The energy of the tango is its beauty and the energy flows from the disappearance of the two individuals to create a third person.

In the dance there are no instructions, no master-servant dynamic. Obedience is not an issue because selflessness is the foundation. There is no one who has to be served, no preferential partner, no clash of wills where one has to submit to the other, but there is a partnership of togetherness that serves the creative expression rather than the individual ability. No wonder the church fathers used the word *perichoresis* as a metaphor to illustrate the being of God. It is a Greek word composed from the word *peri* (around) and *choreo,* from which our word choreography comes—to move or dance around.

Come Dance With Me

The real good news is that the death of Jesus has opened the way into the dance. For eternity the dance was invisible, but the Word God spoke in Christ manifested the dance in the flesh. As a Man, Jesus came to show us how the tango should be danced with an unseen Partner. Jesus came to showcase a life of humility that does not demand to live its own life but is satisfied to live the life of another. The humility that brings about the kind of attentiveness and freedom from crowd-pleasing that made Him the perfect dance partner.

Jesus prayed that we would be extended an open invitation to enter into the dance:

> *I do not pray for these alone, but also for those who will believe in Me through their word; that they all may be one, as You, Father, are in Me, and I in You; that they also may be one in Us, that the world may believe that You sent Me. And the glory which You gave Me I have given them, that they may be one just as We are one: I in them, and You in Me; that they may be made perfect in one, and that the world may know that You have sent Me, and have loved them as You have loved Me* (John 17:20-23 NKJV).

We have become the dance partners and the whole plan of redemption is depending on how we dance; *"that they may be perfect in one and that the world may know...."* We have been invited and empowered to be the fourth partner in the eternal tango of love. This is our real witness; not soapbox preaching or grandstanding in the faith, but our love for one another and for our Partner.

It is love that transforms us from onlookers and by-standers to participants. The God-dance is a manifestation of the Being of God and as such can be nothing more or less than movement soaked in love. This is what we all crave—to be loved—and this is where we find it—in the dance. In the movement we find out with absolute certainty that He loves us as He loves Jesus and that He is much more committed to the intimacy that perfects the dance than we are. In interacting with this God and moving close with total abandonment, we are drawn into the pre-existent love story that has been the motivation for writing the whole drama of creation.

In interacting with this God and moving close with total abandonment, we are drawn into the pre-existent love story that has been the motivation for writing the whole drama of creation.

Just like a beginner who is being taught to dance the tango, the qualification for the dance cannot be perfection but the enthusiasm of the student who loves to be taught and who loves the dance. We do not join the class because we are coerced into it by some wild-eyed evangelist adept in the four spiritual laws; we join because we have seen the end result in someone else and desire is birthed in us. We join because we desire expression of self and we continue because we discover the expression of a joined life that is born out of intimacy, activity, adventure, and discovery—the expression of a third person. As we grow in the ability to lay down our own desire for expression and are consumed by a desire to express the new identity, we are swept up into a new joy—not the joy of self-realization, but the joy of Christ-realization.

There is no place here for judgment or for performance or score cards. No place for obedience to rules and instructions. We do not dance in a competition; we dance because we love the dance. Only the dance matters, and we continuously discover deeper possibilities of abandonment to each other, deeper intimacy, and the prospect of producing something that is so desirable that it will draw others to make the same commitment—to the dance.

And while we dance, we don't shout instructions to one another. The only communication is the shared life of our commitment to one another and to the dance. There may be soft words of love or encouragement, but the focus is on an inner communication—deeds without words. This is not the time to remember or communicate rules; this is the time to feel and to respond. There is no sense of responsibility, just a desire to respond to one another. The only real expectation when you get to this stage of the dance is that you will expect nothing from one another except to be given over to the rhythm and to each other. It is all response and no responsibility.

This is the most difficult part of learning the deep secrets of the tango. Because there has to be total selflessness, the humility to be led, total focus on your partner, and abandonment to another person, and it only comes with time and much dancing.

We don't just walk away from self and into the communal experience without being willing to spend time and effort. Yes, there is effort, but the goal of the effort is not perfect technique, it is abandonment. This is not learnt from *Tango for Dummies*, it is acquired by spending hours with your partner on the dance floor.

The only striving required is what is needed to enter into the rest of selfless abandonment to the minutest nuances of the expression of your partner. Perfection is impossible if you try to dance according to the rules. For the untrained eye you may perform as well as the Pharisees and your religious efforts may be applauded by thousands and enjoyed by the crowds, but you will know and He will know. In the end, your dance will not be an invitation to others but a showpiece of effort—and who needs more effort these days? We need love, enthusiasm, abandonment, and transcendence. Perfection is not the ideal medium for that. A friendship that has prepared us for communication that transcends even words forms the perfect background for a breathtaking adventure in love and abandonment.

And our Friend is asking, "May I have this dance?"

ENDNOTES

1. C. Baxter Krueger, *The Parable of the Dancing God* (Jackson, MS: Perichoresis Press, 1994), 33.

2. Qtd. in Brennan Manning, *The Signature of Jesus* (Portland, OR: Multnomah Press, 1992), 144.

3. Ibid., 144.

4. Brother Lawrence, *The Practice of the Presence of God* (New Kensington, PA: Whitaker House, 1982), 87.

5. Ibid., 65

6. Oswald Chambers, *My Utmost for His Highest* (Vereeniging, South Africa: Christian Art Publishers, 1993), February 11.

7. Frank Laubach, *Letters by a Modern Mystic* (Syracuse, NY: New Readers Press, 1955), 7

8. Dr. William R. Long on his blog 17/05/06 © 2004-2008 www.drbilllong.com.

CHAPTER 7

The Wisdom and Power of Intimacy

GARY WIENS

In the late 1980s, the Lord began to stir my heart toward prayer in a significant way. At the time, it seemed as though what was going on inside me was nothing more than a jumbled confusion of thoughts and feelings rooted in my pastoral ministry experience, which was coming upon difficult times. I was beginning to feel drawn into a more focused and intimate place of prayer, and it was very unsettling to me because I knew of no context of ministry in which this type of prayer could happen in more than a marginal way.

During that season, the Lord began to draw me toward the writings of historical contemplatives such as St. John of the Cross, Teresa of Avila, Jeanne Guyon, and others. It was also during this season that I began hearing the whispers of the Holy Spirit concerning "Marys of Bethany"—people who would someday join the ministry to which I was being called. I really had no idea who these people were or why they would come. This impression seemed like nothing more than a vague breath of information from the Spirit, about which I could do nothing.

Since 1999, it has been my privilege to be associated with the International House of Prayer in Kansas City, Missouri. During this time, I have come to understand to a greater degree these faint murmurings of the Spirit of God. The Marys of Bethany began to come, and a significant group of intercessory worshipers has gathered in Kansas City to spend their lives ministering to the Lord and coming to agreement concerning His agenda for that city and for the cities and nations of the earth. These individuals are male and female, married and single, old and young. Their hearts burn with one primary passion—to love the Lord their God with all their heart, soul, mind, and strength. With a fiery zeal they want to love what He loves and pray for the salvation of human beings all over the world.

This may sound very exciting, especially to those who have a similar sense of vocation smoldering in their breast. But in the contemporary evangelical church of our day, it is difficult for those whose hearts pulsate with this sense of calling to feel like anything but square pegs trying to fit in round holes. The reason for this, I believe, is that today's Church in the Western world is consumed with activism. We adhere to a "go" doctrine, rooted in the expectation of effective performance and results-oriented ministry activity. Therefore, the idea of giving oneself vocationally to a place of contemplation that may not yield short-term, immediate results is a concept that often meets with skepticism at best and outright rejection at worst. My hope is to face this mind-set head-on in this chapter and attempt to bring validation and understanding regarding the ministry of extravagant lovers of God.

THE WISDOM OF EXTRAVAGANT PRAYER

Near the end of Jesus' public ministry, He told a parable that holds significant meaning for us today. It is the parable of the ten virgins, found in the twenty-fifth chapter of the Gospel of Matthew:

Then the Kingdom of Heaven shall be likened to ten virgins who took their lamps and went out to meet the bridegroom. Now five of them were wise, and five were foolish. Those who were foolish took their lamps and took no oil with them, but the wise took oil in their vessels with their lamps. But while the bridegroom was delayed, they all slumbered and slept. And at midnight a cry was heard: "Behold, the bridegroom is coming; go out to meet him!" Then all those virgins arose and trimmed their lamps. And the foolish said to the wise, "Give us some of your oil, for our lamps are going out." But the wise answered, saying, "No, lest there should not be enough for us and you; but go rather to those who sell, and buy for yourselves." And while they went to buy, the bridegroom came, and those who were ready went in with him to the wedding; and the door was shut. Afterward the other virgins came also, saying, "Lord, Lord, open to us!" But he answered and said, "Assuredly, I say to you, I do not know you." Watch therefore, for you know neither the day nor the hour in which the Son of Man is coming (Matthew 25:1-13 NKJV).

This parable instructs us in several ways concerning the extravagant pursuit of intimacy with Jesus through prayer. First of all, it is one of the final public words Jesus spoke, given only a few days before His crucifixion and death. We can presume that if Jesus knew He was coming to the end of His life, He would speak about the things closest to His heart. In this case, Jesus speaks from the bridal paradigm, and His topic is the marriage celebration of the Bridegroom and the Bride! He likens the Kingdom of Heaven to the expected return of the groom to claim his wife and builds this parable around the events associated with that return.

Second, it is important to notice that Jesus is speaking here about an important contrast—the difference between the "wise" and the "foolish" virgins. The virgins in the story are the wedding party attendants. They are fully focused on the return of the bridegroom, and they speak to us in symbolic fashion of individuals or churches who have understood the message of the coming of the Lord and of His passionate love for His Bride. They have heard the call of the Holy Spirit, their hearts are turned toward the Lord, and they are eagerly awaiting His return.

They have heard the call of the Holy Spirit, their hearts are turned toward the Lord, and they are eagerly awaiting His return.

Each attendant carries a lamp, which may be interpreted as referring to the ministry each virgin represents. In the book of Revelation, the

Lord Jesus speaks to John the apostle about the lamps of the churches and about what the churches must do to have their lamps—their effective ministries—restored to full authority and influence. Collectively, these virgins make up the Bride of Christ, and they are called individually to know the depth of that identity.

It is important to see that this is not a parable that builds a contrast between those who are saved at the end of the age and those who are cast out of the Kingdom of God. The contrast is not between "holy" and "wicked" people, but between those who are "wise" and "foolish," and the difference between the two groups is not their doctrine or their methodology. The contrast consists of one essential thing: At the crucial moment of the story, when the call goes out that the bridegroom is coming, five of the virgins have oil for their lamps and five of them do not.

The "oil" in this parable speaks to us of the fuel for ministry, which causes the light of the Gospel to burn brightly before the eyes of the watching world. That fuel is the combustible reality of a fresh and intimate relationship with Jesus Christ through the ministry of the Holy Spirit. Consider this brief reference from *The New Unger's Bible Dictionary:*

> "Oil was a fitting symbol of the Spirit or spiritual principle of life, by virtue of its power to sustain and fortify the vital energy; and the anointing oil, which was prepared according to divine instructions, was therefore a symbol of the Spirit of God, as the principle of spiritual life that proceeds from God and fills the natural being of the creature with the powers of divine life. Anointing with oil, therefore, was a symbol of endowment with the Spirit

of God for the duties of the office to which a person was consecrated."[1]

When the story begins, all ten virgins have enough oil in their lamps to meet the normal expectations of the day. The bridegroom is scheduled to come, the call has gone forth, and the preparations have been made. The lamps are all burning brightly, and the atmosphere is festive with gleeful anticipation. Then a significant factor is introduced into the story. It is the matter of *strategic delay*. The bridegroom does not come when he is expected. As a matter of fact, by the expectations of the wedding party, he is very late, so late that all the members of the wedding party become weary and fall asleep.

In my observation, as one involved in church life for decades, one of the most surprising realities of the Christian experience and one for which most believers are not well prepared is that of strategic delay as a tool in the hand of God. Human beings, especially those of us who live in the digital world of instant and constant communication and production, expect the events of our lives to occur speedily and according to a predictable timetable.

Almost nothing makes us more nervous than not having a clear sense of when something is going to happen. When God decides to introduce a strategic delay into the equations of our lives, it can be disorienting and disturbing. While we Westerners are more prone to this sort of confusion than our Eastern brothers and sisters, this parable makes it clear that the virgins, too, had an expectation of the timing of this event. The fact is clear that the bridegroom's delay was much longer than any of them had projected, and only half of them had prepared adequately for such an eventuality.

The five virgins called "wise" are so designated by Jesus because they have taken the time to collect extra oil. These five represent those in the Body of Christ who are enamored with the Person of Jesus not so much because He will strengthen their ministry, but because they are in love with *Him*. In the symbolic interpretation of this text, the wise group has taken the time to cultivate a deeper relationship of intimacy with the Lord beyond the day-to-day function of their ministries. They have established the pattern of developing intimacy with Jesus *as an end in itself*, rather than as the means to effective ministry. Regardless of their external circumstances, this internal reward is the motivating factor of their lives.

Those who are "foolish" have only taken time to fill their lamps for the expected activities of the day, without provision for an unexpected delay. It is my conviction that this "foolish virgin" pattern of operating is one of the chief weaknesses of believers today. In spite of an awareness that our lives cannot be effective and fulfilling without the blessing and anointing of the Holy Spirit, the goal still is not intimacy with Jesus, but rather achieving success in our chosen fields of endeavor. This dilemma extends even to those who give themselves to vocational ministry in the Body of Christ. We become "brokers" of the Word and the Spirit, men and women who study the Scriptures and pray, *not* because of a passion for intimacy with the Man Christ Jesus, but because we have to preach a sermon or teach a lesson or prepare for a discipleship group. In the language of the parable, we have oil enough for our lamps to burn, but nothing in reserve to sustain us during an unexpected delay. Again, please note that this is not about wickedness, but about foolishness as opposed to wisdom.

We become "brokers" of the Word and the Spirit, men and women who study the Scriptures and pray, *not* because of a passion for intimacy with the Man Christ Jesus, but because we have to preach a sermon or teach a lesson or prepare for a discipleship group.

The coming of the Bridegroom is delayed without regard for the relative level of preparation. The day stretches into the evening, and then into late evening. All the virgins become weary of waiting and fall asleep. Suddenly, at midnight, the cry rings out: *The bridegroom is coming!* Everyone scrambles to alertness, bustling about to get ready for the celebration of His joyous arrival.

This is when the foolish virgins make a terrifying discovery—their lamps have run out of oil. They realize with horror that they cannot participate in the festivities without oil in their lamps. Their first thought is to go to the wise virgins and borrow some oil. They are flatly refused and told to get their own from the merchants.

This seems quite a harsh posture on the part of the wise women, but it is eminently understandable as we grasp the meaning of what is being said. The truth is simply that one individual cannot give to another the relationship of intimacy that has been cultivated with Jesus over weeks, months, and years. There is nothing more personal than one's own place of intimacy with one's beloved, and try as we might, we cannot "borrow" from someone else's depth of relationship. I might look with envy at the life of one of these people and desire to emulate their pattern of cultivating relationship with Christ, but I cannot have their life in God. I must cultivate that on my own.

The foolish five are faced with this reality and they become aware that the only course of action is for them to go to the merchants and buy their own oil. In other words, they must go and invest the time and energy necessary to cultivate intimacy with Jesus for its own sake.

Why is this critical? I believe that during the "strategic delay" that faces the Body of Christ at the end of the age, there is emerging an increasing influence of darkness and trouble that will try the very foundations of our faith in God. Evil is rampant and the darkness is getting darker. The Lord of hosts is preparing to become involved in a significant way in bringing justice to the earth in the form of His temporal judgments, and these judgments will be terrible in their force and their effectiveness. Judgment is rooted in the jealous heart of the Bridegroom God and has as its purpose the removal of all barriers to bridal love.

But the sober reality is that the judgments of God will affect many believers as well as unbelievers in negative ways. Everyone will experience the coming troubling circumstances—natural disasters, weather situations, wars, diseases, and human violence. All of these things will be used in the sovereign power of God to work justice in the earth and to defeat the powers of darkness that hinder the people of God from loving Him as He deserves.

I know many intercessors who have grown weary in the waiting, skeptical that the promises will be fulfilled, because their eyes are focused on the resolution of issues rather than on the Person of Jesus. Their goal is the realization of prophetic promises instead of deepening intimacy with Jesus, and thus their reward remains external. When the fulfillment of their dreams and promises is delayed, discouragement and weariness take their toll.

By contrast, those whose hearts are rooted and grounded in the love of Jesus and whose relationship is focused on intimate friendship with Him have the resources to stand strong. They can discern the ways of the Lord and become His partners in the activity of loosing blessing and judgment on the earth. Their focus is not on the realization of an external promise. They know experientially that He is the fullness of every promise, and in His sweet kiss upon the heart their joy is made full.

Jesus and His Father God, through this time of strategic delay, will bring the peoples of the earth to the point at which His intervention is absolutely necessary. He will orchestrate the timing of that intervention to bring maximum glory to His own Name. Those who have oil in abundance, who have cultivated intimacy with Jesus by the Holy Spirit, will understand with a much greater degree of peace and rest what His strategies are and will find the grace to cooperate with them.

Those who have only enough oil for the day-to-day function of their ministries may find themselves in a dry state, having lost their effectiveness. Their lamps will go out, and they will miss the celebration enjoyed by those who have entered the intimate place. This is what I believe the parable means when, at the very end, the foolish virgins are turned away at the door. I do not believe this speaks of eternal judgment, but rather of being turned away from sharing as partners with Christ in the celebration of the Bridegroom's joyful activity when He returns to establish His Kingdom on the earth at the end of the age.

THE WISDOM OF INTIMACY

In the goodness of God, He has given us a real-life story in which the people involved live out this reality before our eyes. I began this chapter by speaking of the "Marys of Bethany" who today are being drawn by the Holy Spirit, and it is the story of Mary of Bethany and her siblings, Martha and Lazarus, that provides the context for understanding Jesus' parable. We can learn much from this story if we have ears to hear.

The story begins with the familiar recounting of Jesus' visit to Martha's home:

> *Now it happened as they went that He entered a certain village; and a certain woman named Martha welcomed Him into her house. And she had a sister called Mary, who also sat at Jesus' feet and heard His word. But Martha was distracted with much serving, and she approached Him and said, "Lord, do You not care that my sister has left me to serve alone? Therefore tell her to help me." And Jesus answered and said to her, "Martha, Martha, you are worried and troubled about many things. But one thing is needed, and Mary has chosen that good part, which will not be taken away from her"* (Luke 10:38-42 NKJV).

Jesus comes to visit His friends, and it is evident that He enjoys their company. Martha, who is dearly loved by Jesus, is the prototypical task-oriented servant. She is so engaged in serving that she is "distracted" by it. Mary, on the other hand, gives herself to sitting at the feet of Jesus, hearing His word. From a human standpoint, there is much to be done. There is much serving, "preparations that had to be made," and Martha is giving herself to those tasks with her customary vigor. Mary is not being helpful to her sister, but rather is focused on what Jesus has to say.

One must have a certain perspective in order to comprehend the importance of what is going on here. The living God is sitting in the house of this little family, on a real day in history. He is encountering real people, just as He comes by the Spirit to encounter you and me today. *The eternal Word of the Father, the Word of God made flesh, is in the front room, and He is in the mood to talk!*

That is a staggering reality! We have become so inured, so accustomed to this kind statement in the Bible that we tend to miss the power of it. The incarnate Christ is encountering human beings. Because of the eternal nature of His word, He is also encountering me if I will turn aside and listen. The bush is still burning, and God Himself will speak to those who come and see. One of those people has the wisdom to sit at His feet and listen to what God is saying to her, while the other has too much to do. Martha is distracted from true wisdom by doing things for God, while Mary makes the choice to hear Him and be drawn into His life.

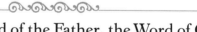

The eternal Word of the Father, the Word of God made flesh, is in the front room, and He is in the mood to talk!

It's important for us to see that, in Martha's eyes, Mary is the foolish one in the beginning of this story. Those who take the time to cultivate intimacy are at first seen as the foolish, the distracted, the unrealistic. They are viewed as those who have lost their grip on reality. "What do they *do*, after all? You mean, you just sit in this House of Prayer and think about God?"

I am struck by how often the question comes: "What results have you seen in the community since you began the House of Prayer?" Now, I understand this question, because there is a focus on prayer for revival in our cities. But the first commandment must come to hold first place in our hearts if anything is going to be established in the truth of the Kingdom. I must settle in my own heart that Jesus is worthy of my love and affection, of my extravagant ministry to Him, *just because He is worthy!*

Make no mistake, there will be community impact, but it is because *He loves the community*, not solely because we are praying that He will do things. The evangelization of our cities is not the first order of business—worship is! John Piper makes this claim so boldly in his marvelous book, *Let The Nations Be Glad*. He states in the introduction that missions are not the ultimate goal of the church. Worship is. Missions exist because worship doesn't.[2] The horizontal effect of prayer is not the first thing on the heart of God! Loving and glorifying His Son is the first order, and without that, nothing else counts!

The Marys of Bethany still are seen as foolish in the eyes of many, but I tell you, it is they who are wise. The Psalmist wrote a powerful song that speaks to this reality:

> *Now therefore, be wise, O kings; be instructed, you judges of the earth. Serve the Lord with fear, and rejoice with trembling. Kiss the Son, lest He be angry, and you perish in the way, when His wrath is kindled but a little. Blessed are all those who put their trust in Him* (Psalms 2:10-12 NKJV).

Be wise, peoples of the earth, and rejoice with trembling. Kiss the Son, lest He be angry and you perish in the day of the kindling of His wrath! It is wisdom to kiss the Son of God, to sit before Him and gaze upon His beauty, to hear Him and gain His perspective on what is right and true. He is worthy, He is lovely, and in His presence there is fullness of joy forever.

Martha doesn't understand. She is focused on her ministry. She has enough oil for the day, enough energy to do her ministry, and she is mostly satisfied (although she would like a little more help!). Mary's heart burns for more than that, and Jesus' response to Martha's indignation is that Mary has chosen the better part—*the one necessary thing*—and it will not be taken from her.

With this the story seems to end, leaving us with a rather unresolved feeling. Those who are like Mary find in this story a good deal of vindication, and those who are more like Martha feel rebuked but don't know how to bring closure to the issues. It has been helpful to me to not look at the story in too much of an individualized fashion, but to see it in a holistic way. In other words, this is not so much about being a Mary or a Martha. Rather, in the household of faith there are those like Mary and those like her sister, and we must understand the importance of doing first things first so that the secondary things can be done with effectiveness and joy. Jesus was not telling Martha that her ministry was invalid. He was saying that there is a first thing without which the second things will burn us out. I don't think Martha understood that yet, but the story was not complete.

It's in the eleventh chapter of John's Gospel that Jesus' involvement with Martha and Mary picks up again. The text is lengthy so it is not included here, but I will summarize the story as it un-folds. Jesus receives word from Mary and Martha that Lazarus, the younger brother of the sisters, is sick. Implicit in the message is the expectation that Jesus will come and heal him.

At this point, God's "strategic delay" is introduced into this real-life situation. The sisters need help, and they need it now. Their brother is sick and dying, and they need the Lord to come *now*. They don't need a sermon or a prayer. They need an inter-vention by God Almighty, and upon hearing the request, Jesus does the absolutely unthinkable thing—*nothing!* His decision is motivated by love for His friends, and by the desire to reveal the glory of God in a maximum way. So He does nothing, and that decision embodies the dramatic dilemma of the strategic delay. Everything in the realm of common sense points to the logic of an immediate intervention—He loves these people, He is within walking distance, He has the power to speak from anywhere and bring healing, they are begging Him to come. He does none of it. He just waits.

There seemingly are no answers available, be-cause in fact the true answer lies outside the realm of human possibility!

Why? My soul feels the tension of this as I write it. *Oh, God, why? Where are You? I need You now, not tomorrow! Why don't you hear my cry?* All of these emotions and more must have gone on in the hearts of Martha and Mary, their friends, and the disciples. What is Jesus doing? Why is He not doing anything? There seemingly are no an-swers available, *because in fact the true answer lies outside the realm of*

human possibility! God is getting ready to do something at the end of the strategic delay that will absolutely rock their world, that will set in motion cataclysmic events, that will turn a village upside-down and bring infinitely more glory to the Name of Jesus than would a mere healing. His plan is so outrageous that the human mind cannot conceive of it. When Jesus made His decision to go to Bethany *more than four days late* in the view of the sisters, the worst-case scenario had in fact happened. Lazarus was dead.

The biblical text tells us that as Jesus enters the town Martha comes to meet Him, but Mary stays in the house. Here is already a picture of the comparative peace resting upon the two women. Martha, in her busyness and anxiety, at least knows where to go. She is, in this story, like the widow of Luke 18. She is precious to God, but her soul is disquieted and confused. Seeking some understanding, she goes to the Lord and brings, as a prayer, a very simple statement: *"Lord, if You had been here, my brother would not have died"* (John 11:21 NKJV). Her level of intimacy with Jesus—her depth of comprehension regarding His ways—is limited, and therefore all she can conceive of as real is what seems obvious. Lazarus has died; therefore the story is over. That's all there is.

One can only pause for a moment to feel the human anguish of that scene, the confusion and accusation that must have been in her heart as she faced the One who had the power to change things and had chosen not to do so. Do you know that place of near madness? How do we stand in such a place with any kind of faith? A God who can do something and does not. It is a major dilemma.

Jesus responds to her with tenderness and begins to comfort her with words of truth about the situation. He promises her that Lazarus will be raised from the dead, but all she can think of is right doctrine, and she refers to the resurrection at the end of the age. But Jesus responds with unimaginable words: *"I am the resurrection and the life. He who believes in me, though he may die, he shall live"* (John 11:25 NKJV).

Jesus personalizes the doctrine and announces to Martha that its fulfillment is standing in front of her. And she still doesn't get it! You see, she still has not taken the time to get past the doctrine to the Person who fulfills the doctrine—the living Word of God. The Resurrection is standing in front of her and she does not recognize Him because she has not cultivated the ability to see with faith. I imagine the eyes of Jesus boring into Martha's soul at that moment, searching for the light of faith that will quicken something inside His heart and release Him to do what He longs to do. But He does not find it in her. Martha's lamp has gone out. Jesus turns from her, leaving her standing at the door, a foolish virgin with no oil in a time of darkness. She will have no immediate partnership in what He is about to do.

Jesus asks for Mary. She is in the house, in a place of rest and peace knowing in the midst of her grief that her Beloved will come when it is time. Her quietness is supra-rational, not something she can easily explain, but in the midst of all the pain and confusion, Mary is at rest! Anxiety does not rule the day with her, because she has come to know the Man Christ Jesus, and she has confidence that in His time He will come and do what needs to be done. Her lamp burns brightly *in the midst of God's strategic delay,* and her faith is not shaken. Is there tension and confusion in her heart? Of course there is! She's a human being with all the passionate emotions that anyone would have in such a circumstance. But she has successfully waged the violent war of chosen trust in a Savior whose character is worthy of her trust, even when she can't understand what He's doing.

When Jesus calls for her, she goes to meet Him and *utters the exact prayer that Martha has spoken moments earlier.* This seems so significant to me. Mary's prayer and Martha's are exactly the same, but the power is not in the words spoken; rather, it is in the depth of relationship behind the words.

Today, many who are caught in the widow's mentality of intercession are focused on praying exactly the right way—binding this, loosing that—and beloved, I tell you it is not about that! It's about the authority of intimacy. Mary understood that fact, and the prayer of her *heart* did the loosing that was necessary, unlocking the power of God in a way that no one except Jesus could anticipate.

The power is not in the words spoken; rather, it is in the depth of relationship behind the words.

The text tells us that when Mary speaks those words, Jesus sees her weeping, and something is released in His inner Being. He groans in His Spirit and is troubled or agitated. His Spirit begins to roll and tumble, brooding over the chaos of the moment, waiting for the right time to utter the word of power. Then He asks for information concerning the location of Lazarus' tomb and goes to do the impossible.

What is so gripping to me about this story is that *it was the weak and confused prayer of Jesus' intimate friend that loosed resurrection power from His Spirit.* I have mused upon this scenario and the different ways the scene could have unfolded. If I were the Messiah, I might have come into Bethany with a fanfare of trumpets blazing forth as I strode down the path to where Lazarus was, doing my best Charlton Heston impersonation. After all, this is God in the flesh, coming to do the impossible. What a scene! The papers would have loved it, and the fame of His Name would have spread through the land!

Jesus' mode of operation, though, is not to show off, but to call His friend, His bridal partner, one with whom He has shared the secrets of His heart, to His side. He has given *her* the authority to stir His heart to do the work that needs to be done. He will not do it on His own. He will not do it without His friend. So when Mary prays, when the wise virgin comes to the Bridegroom and whispers her request, the door is opened, all the power of Heaven comes to bear upon the issue of the day and resurrection power is released. The voice of God thunders into the nether regions, the gates of death are shattered by the sound, the breath of God enters once more into a human frame that has been held in the grip of the enemy, and life comes forth from death.

This is *all* released by the power and authority of intimacy. *The intercession of the Bride!* There is no authority like it in Heaven or on the earth.

At the end of the day, the one who seemed foolish at the beginning was found to be wise. And please understand, Martha was blessed as well! She was not sent off in shame to lament her lack of intimacy. She received her brother back as well. But what she missed was the celebration of partnership, the exhilaration of touching the heart of

God with her prayers and seeing Him do in partnership with her what only He can do.

I believe with all my heart that God intends to release a ministry of power in the earth in these last days. The Lazarus generations will be brought forth from the dead through the power of prayer. But that power cannot be released in full measure to the widow-like intercessors whose hearts are filled with right doctrine but who know little intimacy, who have the right lexicon of prayer but whose hearts are weary because they lack a fresh and vital friendship with the Beloved. God is showing Himself to be nearby, not far off. The Bridegroom is in the land, and He has brought His redemption with Him. He has come to Martha's house and He is in the mood to talk, to reveal His ways and means.

Jesus invites you who stand in the place of that precious sister to come aside for a moment and put first things first, to allow the issues and agendas of the day to be set aside for a moment. I am utterly convinced that those who draw near to love Him will find themselves on the receiving end of the earth-shaking power of the living Word, for He cares about those issues and agendas in an infinitely greater way than we do. Jesus talks to His friends so that they might be established in faith, that in the time of delay their hearts will not be shaken and that they might stir the very heart of God with their prayers. They are the wise virgins. What they have chosen will not be taken from them.

ENDNOTES

1. *The New Unger's Bible Dictionary* (Chicago, IL: Moody Press, 1988).

2. Piper John, *Let the Nations Be Glad* (Grand Rapids, MI: Baker Books, 1993), 11.

CHAPTER 8

Intimacy With God: Knowing and Being Known

MARC A. DUPONT

"...Unless you eat the flesh of the Son of Man and drink His blood, you have no life in yourselves" Jesus told to the multitudes at Capernaum (John 6:53 NASB). This statement came at the height of Jesus' popularity during His time on earth prior to the resurrection. Both the number of disciples and the crowds who had been following Him and hanging on every word had been increasing dramatically. Not only due to the power of His words, but also due to the signs and wonders that accompanied Him.

These words of eating His body and drinking His blood turned out to be a publicist's worst nightmare, however. Almost immediately, the crowds went from being desperate to see and hear Him to disappearing altogether. The multitudes went from praising Him to criticizing Him. In fact, even among those who counted themselves disciples of Him (the larger group of disciples), many stopped following Him. Indeed, Jesus even asked the twelve if they were going to leave Him as well (see John 6:67). Peter's response, while affirming their commitment to follow Jesus, also lets us know that the twelve themselves did not really understand the importance of Jesus words.

Today, some two millennia later, we symbolically eat a small piece of bread and take a sip of grape juice in remembering that Jesus, the Bread of Life, gives us a spiritual nourishment beyond what any food or drink in the natural can provide. But do we really understand why Jesus deliberately spoke of Himself in such a perplexing way that was sure to cause confusion and disbelief?

RADICAL INTIMACY

Scientists used to say that the human body replaces each cell, of the replaceable ones, every seven years or so. Today, most scientists do not agree on any particular timeline since learning that the molecules and subatomic particles of the body can move within themselves at the speed of light. However, most would be in agreement that, in essence, you become what you eat. Morgan Spurlock, who did the *Super-Size Me* documentary, ate at McDonald's restaurants every day for 30 days. After a month of eating junk food, he gained 14 pounds, began to experience psychological mood swings, and did damage to his liver. In eating junk food every day, his body and even his mind became somewhat junk!

When Jesus spoke those enigmatic words that to some seemed demonic in origin, He was actually making a most amazing and almost unbelievable statement. His words were heard but not truly heard, because the goodness of what He was communicating was beyond our perceptions of love and good. In essence, He was saying that He, God Himself, wants to be so much a part of our lives that He is like the food we eat that actually over time not only nourishes us but replaces those replaceable cells within us! He was speaking parabolically in order to catch the attention of his listeners—then, now, and throughout the ages of the church!

WORDS OF TRANSCENDENCE

Damah is one of the basic Hebrew words for "parable" (see Hosea 12:10).[1] A true *damah* consists of three aspects. First, there is the known part. In all the parables Jesus told, there was always a common focus point that was familiar to everyone of His day. His common word pictures were of things of planting, harvesting, fishing, losing a coin, et cetera. The second aspect of *damah* is something that is either unknown or at least strange when joined with the known within the story, song, or picture. When those two elements are combined, especially when inspired by the Holy Spirit, the result is transcendence, or change, which is the third element.

Eating and drinking was, and is, such a common and completely necessary part of daily life. And in many cultures, if not most, eating and drinking are viewed as much more than a simple necessity. It is upheld as an art and even a celebration for many. It is one of the few things that every human being has in common—without eating and drinking, we begin to deteriorate and then eventually die!

By parabolically combining this everyday necessity of eating and drinking with what was despised in the Hebrew culture—cannibalism—Jesus was trying to convey God's radical heart for intimacy in a radical way. A way that would stumble people enough to make them really explore this strange *damah*.

The unanswered question for most, and even the unasked question for many, is "If there is a God, how much does He want to be involved in my life?" For those who have come to the revelation that Jesus, the Christ, gave His life on the Cross so that we might again actually know God, this question is the burning bush before us. The immediate question we need to ask our selves is, *"Are we willing to turn aside, as Moses did, and ascend the hill of the Lord"* in order to know God more intimately? (See Exodus 3:3.) The fact that you are reading this book indicates you are, indeed, willing!

FAITH IN WHAT OR WHOM?

In John 6, prior to Jesus' startling statement that one must eat of His body and drink of His blood, Jesus was asked, "What are the works that one must do?" He responded: *"This is the work of God, that you believe in Him whom He has sent"* (John 6:29 NKJV). Faith, while not the most essential thing in the Kingdom of God, is a very important key. The Book of Hebrews tells us, *"Without faith it is impossible to please **Him**, for he who comes to God must believe that He is, and **that** He is a rewarder of those who seek Him"* (Heb. 11:6 NKJV).

As important as faith is, however, it is not the end in and of itself. Rather, it is the doorway that allows us access to the Person and love of God.

As important as faith is, however, it is not the end in and of it-self. Rather, it is the doorway that allows us access to the Person and love of God. For many, their faith rests in the promises and precepts of God. However important that level of faith is, if the promises and precepts of God are not seen as the characteristics and nature of God, as opposed to the actual Person of God, then all can be lost even though a level of blessing can be experienced. For example, one can have faith that God wants to heal someone of a disease and be a vessel that God uses for healing but still miss the bigger picture of God Himself. In fact, Jesus warned that there actually would be some who would be claim to have been used by God to heal, proph-esy, and deliver, but the Lord would say to some of them *"I never knew you"* (see Matt. 7:23)! The word "knew" in that context is the Greek word *ginosko* which means to know with the implication of a growing sort of knowledge as in a relationship, as opposed to simply knowing in a factual sense.[2] The implication of Jesus' words are that one can have faith in the things of God but come up short in the relationship department.

The all-consuming faith that God calls us to walk in is more than simply believing in the truths about God. And He also calls us to have faith for more than what happened on the Cross two thousand years ago. The first chapter of the Book of Ephesians contrasts two levels of faith. The first is what could be called a foundational faith. It reads, *"In Him, you also, after listening to the message of truth, the gospel of your salvation—having also **believed**, you were sealed in Him with the Holy Spirit of promise"* (Eph. 1:13 NASB). This is a faith for the follower of Christ, which in a sense is past tense. It was the exercise of faith when our hearts first became aware of the reality of the gospel and, through the operation of that faith, became born again into the family of God. Verses 17-19 speak of a differing level of faith—a progressive faith, if you will. It speaks of a continual exercise of faith toward the Person of God the Father in a dynamic relationship as opposed to a static relationship:

> *That the God of our Lord Jesus Christ, the Father of glory, may give to you a spirit of wisdom and of revelation in the knowledge of Him.* **I pray that** *the eyes of your heart may be enlightened, so that you will know what is the hope of His calling, what are the riches of the glory of His inheritance in the saints, and what is the surpassing greatness of His power toward us who believe...* (Ephesians 1:17-19 NASB).

That last word of the quotation, "believe," is not denoting the past-tense faith of verse 13. It is rather a present active participle, which is a formal way of saying an active and ongoing faith in the Person of God within the context of a vital relationship with God.

The heart of Ephesians 1:17-19 is the apostle Paul's heart for all Christians to experientially know and be engaged with the Person of God. This sort of vital relationship with the Person of God is unfortunately not always common in the church today. Rather, like the Hebrews of the Old Covenant, we find it all too easy to trust in religious rituals, sacrifices, and an intellectual knowledge of God rather than daring to believe in the power of the Cross and the all-consuming love of God. It is this sort of faith that God calls us to grow into, develop, and trust in. In short, He calls us to dare to believe that He loves us so deeply that He desires real intimacy with us not mere religious formality.

A common phrase that is used today is the line, "God is into relationship, not religion." The question before us, however, is, "What type of relationship?" A formal relationship of simply being part of a good church? A relationship marked by a change of lifestyle? Or could it be a relationship of intimacy, where whatever changes we go through, our lifestyle and activity flow from the heart within a context of deep love and friendship with God?

I believe the Holy Spirit is continually challenging us to dare to believe that the power of the Cross does not merely result in free fire insurance so that we can escape the pits of hell, but rather that we may truly experience the height, the width, the breadth, and the depth of His amazing love on a personal basis. This ongoing faith in His vast heart for each of us is the real work He calls us to.

Most New Testament scholars believe the apostle Paul to be the primary theologian of all the New Testament writers. In the book of Galatians he wrote:

> *Therefore the Law has become our tutor **to lead us** to Christ, so that we may be justified by faith. But now that faith has come, we are no longer under a tutor. For you are all sons of God through faith in Christ Jesus* (Galatians 3:24-26 NASB).

With huge brush strokes, Paul is making a generalized, sweeping statement that the primary purpose of the Old Covenant is simply to teach us of the impossibility of earning the blessings of God. Isaiah, the prophet, stated *"For all of us have become like one who is unclean, and all our righteous deeds are like a filthy garment…"* (Isa. 64:6 NASB). It is in the Old Covenant that the Law came, which no one can completely live up to. Psalms reads, *"They have all turned aside, together they have* become corrupt; there is no one who does good, not even one" (Ps. 14:3 NASB). And yet, even though much of the message of the Old Testament portion of the Bible speaks of the futility of man to please God by his own efforts, there remain promises and prophesies of a great grace that was yet to come. In fact, a huge portion of the prophetic messages of the Old Testament speak of Jesus, the Grace of God Himself.

A huge portion of the prophetic messages of the Old Testament speak of Jesus, the Grace of God Himself.

Aside from the messianic prophesies, however, the Old Testament Scriptures give hints—even much more than hints—that God, despite the law which He gave, was about grace rather than performance. When Moses ascended the hill of the Lord in Exodus 34, he encountered a bit of the awesome manifest Presence of God. As God passed by, He had Moses stand on a rock with a cut in it, as it were. Even this picture is a prophetic picture of the Rock of our salvation—Jesus, who was pierced for us so that we could again be able to gaze upon God. As the Lord passed by He allowed Moses to see just a bit of His glory. And the then the Lord proclaimed of Himself: *"The Lord, the Lord God, compassionate and gracious, slow to anger, and abounding in lovingkindness and truth"* (Exod. 34:6 NASB). David, the lover of God's Presence, sang, *"For You, Lord, are good, and ready to forgive, and abundant in lovingkindness to all who call upon You"* (Ps. 86:5 NASB). What David and the other prophets knew was that God desired us to experience intimacy with Him. This was something that, prior to the Cross, was impossible for any of us to achieve due to our natural propensities, habits, and appetites in our fallen condition.

After David was confronted by Nathan the prophet for his sin of adultery with Bathsheba and the subsequent murder of her husband, he wrote and sang his famous repentance song of Psalm 51:

> *Create in me a clean heart, O God, and renew a steadfast spirit within me. Do not cast me away from Your presence and do not take Your Holy Spirit from me. Restore to me the joy of Your salvation and sustain me with a willing spirit. Then I will teach transgressors Your ways, and sinners will be converted to You. Deliver me from bloodguiltiness, O God, the God of my salvation; then my tongue will joyfully sing of Your righteousness. O Lord, open my lips, that my mouth may declare Your praise. For You do not delight in sacrifice, otherwise I would give it; You are not pleased with burnt offering. The sacrifices of God are a broken spirit; a broken and a contrite heart, O God, You will not despise. By Your favor do good to Zion; build the walls of Jerusalem. Then You will delight in righteous sacrifices, in burnt offering and whole burnt offering; then young bulls will be offered on Your altar* (Psalms 51:10-19 NASB).

David's song is much more a song of celebration than a funeral dirge. While it is clear David is approaching God from a repentant heart, it is also clear that he is reveling in God's mercy and grace as opposed to a hopeless mourning due to his own failings. Instead of the religious sacrifices of bulls and goats, which the Law demanded, David looked past that to the heart of God. In verse 6 of the psalm

David wrote *"Behold, You desire truth in the innermost being, and in the hidden part You will make me know wisdom"* (Ps. 51:6 NASB). David as a prophet and lover of God knew that God's desire was for something in his life that no amount of religious striving could ever achieve. God desired David to know Him in the depths of David's own heart. After all, the truth is far more than mere precepts and facts. The ultimate truth is the Person of Jesus Himself (see John 14:6).

The call for the contemporary western church is to move beyond the promise of the free fire insurance and transcend into both the friends of God and the intimate lovers of God. It was for this reason that God has placed His very own Spirit within us rather than merely upon us. In all the ages leading up to Jesus giving His life on the Cross, humans could know an anointing of the Holy Spirit upon them, but due to their sinful condition they could not have the Holy Spirit within. Thus the prophets, sometimes the kings, and sometimes the warriors of God would have an anointing—or capacity—of God upon them to serve God and lead His people. For most people, however, there was little real chance of hearing God on a consistent basis. For this reason, the prophets of the Old Covenant times had to be completely correct when prophesying, because the average person simply could not discern the voice of the Lord.

Jeremiah, one of the most powerfully used prophets of God, prophesied something radical about a new covenant that God was going to bring in the future. He said, concerning this new covenant (a relationship of promise and commitment):

> *"Behold, days are coming," declares the Lord, "when I will make a new covenant with the house of Israel and with the house of Judah, not like the covenant which I made with their*

fathers in the day I took them by the hand to bring them out of the land of Egypt, My covenant which they broke, although I was a husband to them," declares the Lord. "But this is the covenant which I will make with the house of Israel after those days," declares the Lord, "I will put My law within them and on their heart I will write it; and I will be their God, and they shall be My people. They will not teach again, each man his neighbor and each man his brother, saying, 'Know the Lord,' for they will all know Me, from the least of them to the greatest of them," declares the Lord, "for I will forgive their iniquity, and their sin I will remember no more" (Jeremiah 31:31-34 NASB).

The implications of this prophecy were enormous. Essentially, Jeremiah was prophesying that the whole Levitical priesthood—a system where only a small portion of God's people could actually know His Presence—would be done away with and that in the future of God's people they could *all know the Lord.* Instead of the everyday person being forced to hear God and know God through a vicarious relationship with a priest or a prophet, all could experience the Person of God.

Instead of the everyday person being forced to hear God and know God through a vicarious relationship with a priest or a prophet, all could experience the Person of God.

In order for the enormity of this prophecy—which was realized through Christ Jesus—to be appreciated, it must be understood that even the Levitical priests, who could come into the Holy Place and the Holy of Holies, and the prophets and kings who had an anointing from God on their lives did not have the Holy Spirit of God dwelling within them. The priests *could* offer up sacrifices for the people and maintain the incense, the lamp, and the Bread of His Presence in the Holy Place. On the Day of Atonement once a year, the High Priest *could* go beyond the Holy Place and into the Holy of Holies where the manifest glory of God was to be found. But for all of that, they could not truly experience day in, day out intimacy with God. The prophets and others, such as some of the kings and warriors, *could* experience God's anointing on their lives at certain times, but they did not have the Spirit of God within them. Rather, there was a resting, or accompanying, gifting of power and wisdom from God on their lives. This anointing, however, was a capacity to serve God rather than the potential for real daily experience of God. Even David, who was so powerfully anointed and used by God, prayed to God, *"Do not cast me away from Your presence and do not take Your Holy Spirit from me"* when he repented of His sin concerning Bathsheba (Ps. 51:11 NASB). Even Moses, the only man that God spoke "mouth to mouth" with, did not have the Spirit of God within him (see Num. 12:8).

The incredible power of the Cross is the complete washing away of all the sins of those who believe in Christ Jesus and what He accomplished on the Cross. This cleansing is so complete that God the Father now sees us as without spot or blemish. He sees our shortcomings as separated from us as the east is from the west. For the first times since the fall of Adam and Eve in the Garden, there is the potential for knowing in a deeply personal way the Person of God. This is the good news! The opportunity of experientially knowing God and being known by Him within a complete context of grace, mercy, and love is available to all. The question, again, is, "Are we willing to take the time and seek the Face of God?" Because true intimacy means far more than knowing about Him and looking forward to the promise of someday going to Heaven. Jesus proclaimed that the Kingdom of God is at hand. And He said to not look for it here or there, but to know it was within us if we began to walk with Him!

THE SCENT OF JESUS

"*...They were amazed, and began to recognize them as having been with Jesus*" (Acts 4:13 NASB). The multitudes recognized something different about Peter and John. It was not their style of clothing or an attitude they projected. It was not clever speech or a certain way of speaking. There was a "Jesus" aroma about these men that simply could not be obtained by anything or anywhere else other than spending time with the Person of God.

Second Corinthians tells us that as we experience the glory of God (His essence) we are transformed or changed by that contact with Him (see 2 Cor. 3:18). Years ago, through doing extensive photographing of newborns in hospitals, they found that even at only a day or two old, those babies would begin to emulate the facial expressions of the parents gazing at them. Ruth Ward Heflin, a renowned Bible teacher, said this:

> There is a greater change that comes about through worship than through any other means. If you want to be changed, worship is the key. When you are worshiping you look into His face and you are changed from glory to glory. We become like that which we worship. We become like Him who we worship.[3]

There comes about a life-giving transformation as we gaze upon, worship, and take in the Person of God. The parabolic eating of Jesus' body and drinking of His blood begins to take on a deeper and more personal meaning as the DNA of our spirits and souls begins to become more Christ-like. We begin to exude the personality of Christ, not through religious striving, but rather simply by being filled with the Holy Spirit and walking with God according to His ways and His will. Saying yes to what we should say yes to and saying no to what we should say no to simply become part of the fruit of the Spirit, as opposed to religious effort and determination on our part. It is at this point that attaining a maturity in Christ Jesus goes from being a religious exercise (which is really Old Covenant performance) to simply the fruit of intimacy with God. We begin to resemble and exude the Person of Christ out of a relationship of intimacy with Him.

The apostle Paul, in his epistle to the church at Ephesus, encouraged them to strive for healthy marriages. He quoted from what God said to Adam (humanity) in the Garden of Eden: *"For this reason a man shall leave his father and mother, and be joined to his wife, and they shall become one flesh"* (Gen. 2:24 NASB). This joining together is at times literal, at times figurative, but most of all it is to be the mind-set of two becoming one and living out life, not only together, but for one another. It is out of the physical joining that babies come forth. It is out of the preferring one another that fulfillment is realized. It is out of the social dynamic of marriage that our identities are to be known, unless one is single, obviously!

Following the Genesis quotation, Paul then shifted gears and went from instructing about healthy marriage to the bigger marriage of that between Christ and His Bride—the Church! Ephesians reads:

"This mystery is great; but I am speaking with reference to Christ and the church" (Eph. 5:32 NASB). Paul, like Jeremiah hundreds of years before, is making a startling statement concerning the degree of relationship God truly desires between Himself and His people!

Without desiring in any way to be coarse, allow me to say God always intended romantic intimacy between a husband and wife to be a sign as to the intimacy that was available between Himself and the people of God. Obviously, we are not speaking about sex here! Rather, we are speaking about the oneness. Not only sharing a journey together, not only sharing a new identity together, but a relationship of knowing one another in a deep, personal, and sacred way that is exclusive of all other relationships. In today's culture, marriage really has little of the connotations that it had even 50 years ago. The brokenness of society is nowhere reflected as much as it is in marriage today and the lack of commitment of spouses one to another and the ensuing lack of commitment to the children of the broken marriages. But in the mind of God, divorce and hardness of heart were never to be part of the marriage scenario. Rather, it was a lifelong commitment "for better or worse," "forsaking all others," not just out of a temporary infatuation with another, but from a lifelong desire to prefer one another to the point of laying down one's life even as Christ did for His Bride.

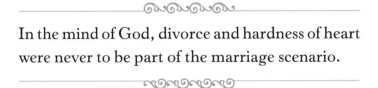

In the mind of God, divorce and hardness of heart were never to be part of the marriage scenario.

My wife and I recently celebrated our twenty-seventh anniversary. We can honestly say that after a quarter of a century of marriage our friendship, commitment, and romance have never been better. Many would ask, "Well, how can that be since you're now in your middle years?" The reason our marriage works so well is not because there have never been tensions or difficulties. The marriage is great because we have continually reminded each other that we came together out of love, and out of the friendship of our love, the intimacy of our love, and the commitment of our love we can go from glory to glory, so to speak, no matter what we have faced!

After 27 years of marriage, rather than feeling disillusioned with one another because we don't look exactly like we did years ago, we tend to laugh more together and find increasingly that our goals, desires, and appetites are so much the same. Why is that? It's simply because out of the years of intimacy and friendship we have deeply impacted and transformed each other. My wife has taught me a great deal about being patient and gracious in relationships. I have, in turn, encouraged her over the years in areas such as faith and risk-taking. There are countless ways in which we have affected one another, but you get the idea.

While Bible study is absolutely vital so that we understand the values and ways of God, it is only through a relationship of intimacy and friendship with God that we can be enabled to walk in His values and ways.

CHOOSING TO BE FILLED

Earlier in the chapter we discussed how the apostle Paul used the Greek word for faith both in the past tense and as a present active participle in his letter to the church of Ephesus. With the former he denoted the past exercise of faith by which those who now belong to

Christ Jesus entered in to the Kingdom of God. With the latter, he wrote of how we can experience the glory of God, know the hope of our calling in Christ Jesus, and know the surpassing greatness of His power toward those who "believe." This very active day-to-day level of faith has a parallel in experiencing day-to-day intimacy with God. In Ephesians 5, he encouraged the church not to be intoxicated with wine or the things of this world, but rather to *"...be filled with the Spirit"* (Eph. 5:18 NASB).

The ongoing filling of the Holy Spirit and walking in the reality of "righteousness, peace, and joy of the Holy Spirit" is always an option available to the believer of Christ Jesus. The question, again, is whether we choose to make a priority of seeking Him. The Bridegroom of the church is not at all dysfunctional or self-absorbed. He is never keeping Himself distant due to having feelings of self-doubt or insecurity. He is never so angry or frustrated with His future Bride that He refuses to spend time with her out of pettiness or pride. He is whole, loving, and completely alive in a way that we cannot even begin to imagine. His relationship with us is always one of constant grace, mercy, compassion, and forgiveness. While it is very true that we can grieve and even offend the Holy Spirit, He is way too healthy to put us off due to pettiness. He is very aware of what we have come out of and the growing pains we go through in unlearning the ways of this world and learning His ways of compassion and truth. This is all to say He is always there, both to receive us and even to promote intimacy with us.

To return for a moment to the idea of marriage being a picture of the intimacy, friendship, and commitment God wants from His people, let's speak just for a moment about nakedness. With a healthy marriage there is just one person in the entire world that a man or woman is naked with. By nakedness I do not mean merely physically, but emotionally and intellectually as well. In the sacredness of the committed relationship of a healthy marriage, there is that one friend and lover with whom we should be free to be vulnerable and transparent with. There should be that one person who will not laugh at your dreams, your tastes, your foibles, or even your physical shape for that matter. In a healthy love, your mate might laugh with you, but never at you to the point of shame or hurt. This is the type of relationship Adam and Eve originally had in the Garden before sin came into the picture. They were whole and free to be who they were without the marring of sin, shame, and guilt. They were free to know each other and God, and free to be known by each other and God. For that reason Genesis 2.25 (NASB) reads, *"The man and his wife were both naked and were not ashamed."* They were free to be real and vulnerable with each other and with God!

How many times have we wanted to pray something out to God, only to turn back by thinking, "Oh, He wouldn't really care about my desire or dream," or, "This is a real need, but I don't know if God really cares that much about me." In the same vein, how many times have our hearts urged us on to go deeper into either worship of God or maybe voicing a prayer of repentance only to think, "Well, I know He really listens to others, but I've failed too many times; He's probably given up on me." All too often, we forfeit the true intimacy God has for us simply by not choosing to believe in the unbelievable goodness of God and His great heart!

All too often, we forfeit the true intimacy God has for us simply by not choosing to believe in the unbelievable goodness of God and His great heart!

One might ask, "What does it feel like to experience intimacy with God? How will I know if I am filled with the Spirit?" In a nutshell, to experience intimacy with God means to experientially know three things. Romans 14 states that the Kingdom of God is *"...righteousness and peace and joy in the Holy Spirit"* (Rom. 14:17 NASB).

First of all, to know the righteousness of God means to know forgiveness of sins to such a degree as to metaphorically be clothed in the righteousness of Christ. It means to be dressed and to be seen in the fine, exquisite robes that the Father of the prodigal son had his son dressed in, rather than the tattered garments he came home in. The fine garments of Heaven are not like the stiff, scratchy, uncomfortable clothing we consider proper or formal. They are garments that radiate the holiness of God but are also cut for fun and adventure. To know the righteousness of God means to know true acceptance and the favor of God the Father, the God of our Lord Jesus Christ! It means to be completely void of all shame, guilt, and condemnation. In short, it means be to experience the very fullness of love, free of all worry or fear (see 1 John 4:18). The imparted righteousness of God in our lives brings a freedom that no human acceptance can ever quite come close to.

It should go without saying that the peace of God is beyond any peace this world can give. It is a peace of mind that no amount of money can buy and no amount of security—as this world measures security—can ever bring about. It is a peace not based on our control or even our understanding of the situation we might be in. It is a supernatural peace that only comes from experiencing the unconditional and all-powerful care and love of God. It is freely ours to know and count on in Jesus Christ due to the power of the Cross. It is a peace that may be greatly at odds with our human perspective of any current difficulties we may be facing. In fact, Jesus told us that in this world we would have tribulation, but to not be afraid. Because He has overcome, He gives us His overcoming peace (see John 14:27).

While there may be trouble without, we can experience complete freedom from fear within! I remember some five years ago, I received what should have been some very startling news via e-mail. My wife and I had invested quite a bit of our savings in an investment group that had, up to that point, had a tremendous history of success. The e-mail indicated that most likely, everything was lost. I remember reading the e-mail late at night thinking that I would let Kim know the bad news in the morning. Surprisingly, I then had a great night's sleep that night. Around 2 P.M. the next day I remembered to tell Kim the bad news. Although both of us were disappointed, we never really did experience any depression or fear of the future due to the loss. In fact, about a week later I thought to myself, "Am I being irresponsible by not feeling more upset about this loss?" While not a huge sum of money to some, the amount did represent quite a bit of savings for us. The truth was, I was not being irresponsible; I was simply experiencing the peace of God that passed all comprehension (see Phil. 4:7).

The third primary characteristic of being intimate with God is experiencing God's supernatural joy. It is a joy completely free of all fear, worry, and insecurity. It is to experientially know the very culture of Heaven. In the Kingdom of God, life is constantly lived at full capacity with joy given and received in every word, gesture, attitude, and action. It is as the state of the sun as described in Psalms: *"Which is as a bridegroom coming out of his chamber; it rejoices as a strong man to run his course"* (Ps. 19:5 NASB).

While long-distance running may seem masochistic to a non-runner, there have been many times I have experienced as a runner where all of a sudden all the training pays off and your body feels like you can simply run forever. It is those runs where, seemingly, your muscles, joints, and lungs are all-powerful, and your running goes from the mundane of training to the joy of being in the state God originally intended.

In the Kingdom of God, life is constantly lived at full capacity with joy given and received in every word, gesture, attitude, and action.

It was a great day of restoration for the Hebrew people when Ezra and the priests read the law to the people of God after 70 years of captivity in Babylon. For decades they had not experienced the freedom of the Word of God being taught to them. As the Word was read and explained to them many began to weep, but Nehemiah the governor said to the people, *"This day is holy to the Lord your God; do not mourn or weep"* (Neh. 8:9 NASB). For all the people were weeping when they heard the words of the law. Then he said to them:

> Go, eat of the fat, drink of the sweet, and send portions to him who has nothing prepared; for this day is holy to our Lord. Do not be grieved, for the joy of the Lord is your strength (Nehemiah 8:10 NASB).

Their default mode, as is ours, was to worship God from a place of shame and doubt concerning His true grace and mercy. In Heaven, however, there is no shame, condemnation, guilt, fear, worry, or insecurity. There is nothing but life abundant. So when Jesus the

King came to express and extend His Kingdom, He said that the thief had come to *"...steal and kill and destroy;* [but] *I came that they may have life, and have it abundantly"* (John 10:10 NASB). A huge part of that abundant life in Him is knowing the radical joy of God's joyful, all-consuming love and care.

THE CALL TO FRIENDSHIP

Over the last two decades, there has been much teaching, preaching, and writing on the Father heart of God and our relationship as His sons. And rightly so. Paul stated, *"You have not received a spirit of slavery leading to fear again, but you have received a spirit of adoption as sons by which we cry out, '**Abba! Father!**'"* (Rom. 8:15 NASB). In our present world culture, the radical increase of broken families has facilitated the increase of the orphan spirit. Another paradigm that has, in recent church history, been rightfully emphasized is that of the church maturing to become the Bride of Christ when Jesus returns.

A third perspective that I believe is essential for the church to grasp and grow into, however, is that of God's desire for friendship with His people. We normally do not think of God wanting to be friends with us, but essentially this faulty thinking is due to three reasons. First, we fail to understand God's desire for intimacy with us. Second, we often fail to realize the prevailing power of the Cross, which makes us acceptable to God. Third, there has been the lack of understanding that God truly loves our humanism.

The orphan spirit, which is rooted in rejection and distrust, especially extends that rejection and distrust toward one's own self. Much of the recent increase in Western culture of self-destructive lifestyles is rooted in self-rejection. That self-rejection and demonic stronghold of viewing ourselves as inherently evil is greatly at odds with God's view and value of us. He sees us as being inherently good due to the fact that we are created in His image. God looked at His creation, including humanity, and said, "It is good!" (See Genesis 1:31.)

On the micro or personal side of things, each human being has been fearfully and wonderfully made. God tells us that even when each of us was in our mother's womb, His hand was upon us in a deeply personal way to make a unique reflection of Himself (see Ps. 139:13-16). God looks at humanity as a whole and sees the potential, no matter what sort of mess we have made of things. He looks at each of us as individuals, no matter how messed up we are, and sees us through eyes of love. In short, God is not anti-human—obviously Jesus Himself is both fully God and fully human. In fact, the Father is so in love with us that He sent His only begotten Son to give His life as a ransom for us. A facet of His love for us is His desire for friendship with each of us.

When I think of friendship and friends, I think of enjoying life! For me to enjoy life I do not necessarily need to be doing something purely fun. I could be working, traveling, eating, relaxing, or just about anything else. A true, mature friendship is not based merely on having fun, but rather the art of enjoying that person and enjoying being with that person no matter what the activity is. The good news is, Jesus calls us to be more than mere servants—He calls us to become His friends.

MANY SERVANTS, FEW FRIENDS

Many yeas ago, I sensed the Lord say to me one day, "I have many servants, but few friends." As I began to think, pray, and explore this statement I began to realize that although we, the church, are far from perfect, God does have many people who are faithful in serving Him. Whether the ministry is teaching Sunday school, evangelism, missions, hosting a small group, or reaching out to the poor, there are countless individuals who are faithful in serving God. That does not mean we don't need more laborers to step up. But what the Lord was really saying was there are few people who desire God simply for being with Him. Mostly when Christians pray, they are praying to gain something. Whether the prayer is a righteous prayer or not is beside the point. Mostly when we pray we are seeking God's hand of provision, protection, or anointing. Whether it is for ourselves or others is moot to the point the Lord wanted to make.

The heart cry of David was simply to know true friendship with the Lord—to be continually in His presence.

In contrast, David, although he prayed for protection, provision, and anointing as well, had his "one thing" prayer. It was the one prayer more than all others he lived for. He prayed in Psalm 27:4:

One thing I have asked from the Lord, that I shall seek: that I may dwell in the house of the Lord all the days of my life, to behold the beauty of the Lord and to meditate in His temple (Psalms 27:4 NASB).

The heart cry of David was simply to know true friendship with the Lord—to be continually in His presence. Jesus told His disciples:

No longer do I call you slaves, for the slave does not know what his master is doing; but I have called you friends, for all things that I have heard from My Father I have made known to you (John 15:15 NASB).

Just as at that point in time with His disciples, so today I believe God is calling many of His servants to continue serving Him, but begin to do so out of a posture of friendship and intimacy.

In the ancient culture, a slave or servant lived a life of constant fear. Their lifestyle was very much one of performance. If they did not perform adequately they might not be fed, or they might be beaten or even sold or killed.

God has never really been interested in a master/slave relationship. Hosea, a prophet, lived and ministered about the same time as Isaiah and Amos. God gave Hosea probably the most unusual instructions found anywhere in Bible. God told him to marry a prostitute as a living parable of His relationship with Israel. Later, after Hosea had redeemed her from a life of shame and loneliness, his wife did the unthinkable— she returned to a lifestyle of prostitution. God then instructed Hosea:

"...Allure her, bring her into the wilderness and speak kindly to her. Then I will give her vineyards from there, and the valley of Achor as a door of hope and she will sing there as in the days of her youth, as in the day when she came up from the land of Egypt. It will come about in that day," declares the Lord, "That you will call Me Ishi and will no longer call Me Baali" (Hosea 2:14-16 NASB).

The rough translation of the last verse is, "You will no longer call Me Master, but rather you will call Me Lover and Friend." Hosea's life and marriage are a picture of God's love for us. A love that, for the most part, we barely know how to return! The heart of God is so rich in mercy, grace, and compassion that we really have no human grid by which to measure His love. As William Cowper wrote, "God is His own interpreter, and he will make it plain."[4]

A friend is someone you share your heart, dreams, and plans with. In calling His disciples to step up into friendship, Jesus made it clear there was going to be an increase in communication about what He was up to. According to the prophets Amos and Isaiah, God does nothing without first revealing it to His prophets (see Amos 3:7; Isa. 42:9). To each of the seven churches Jesus spoke to in the Book of Revelation, He encouraged them to develop ears to hear what the Spirit was saying. He stated to His disciples and to the church that He would send them and us the Holy Spirit who would disclose to us His plans to come! (See John 16:13.)

The key for having ears to hear and eyes to see the things of the Kingdom and what our Heavenly Father is up to is simply intimacy. Intimacy based on God's perfect love, which casts out fear of rejection and punishment. Intimacy which, joined with commitment, obedience, and friendship, becomes a completely consuming, fulfilling, and life-changing relationship. A relationship of incomparable peace, joy, and purpose. The Lord God Jehovah is absolutely amazing in every facet of who He is and in everything He does. The radical good news is that He calls us to dare to believe that we can join Him in the adventure of life—not merely in a formal religious striving, but as the friends, sons, and intimate lovers of God!

ENDNOTES

1. James Strong, *Strong's Exhaustive Concordance of the Bible* (Peabody, MA: Hendrickson Publishers, first published in 1894), ISBN 0-917006-01-1, 1819.

2. *Vine's Expository Dictionary of New Testament Words* (Antioch's Bible Study Tools: http://www.antioch.com. sg/cgibin/bible/vines/get_defn.pl?num=1579).

3. Ruth Ward Heflin, *Glory: Experiencing the Atmosphere of Heaven* (Hagerstown, MD: McDougal Publishing Company, 1996).

4. "Olney Hymns, 'Light Shining out of Darkness," (1779).

Chapter 9

How Ancient Voices Can Deepen Our Relationship With God

Dr. Peter Fitch

Intimacy with God is affected by how we choose to live, but it is also deeply impacted by how we learn to think. Once, after the prophet Jeremiah complained to God about the difficulty of his calling, God responded by saying, *"If you return, then I will restore you—before Me you will stand; and if you extract the precious from the worthless, you will become My spokesman"* (Jer. 15:19 NASB). Heart and mind are both involved in each of these activities, yet "returning" may be seen primarily as a function of the heart. It is something we all must learn to do if we want to develop a deep relationship with God that grows and develops for a lifetime. Whenever we realize that we have drifted away from God in our heart, it is time to return. In a way, the Prodigal Son is a story for everyday. "Extracting the precious from the worthless" is a little different; it mostly involves our thought processes. We are called to be treasure hunters, to look for the good and learn to discard the bad. We need excellent filters in order to build healthy Christian thinking. And it is only from healthy thinking that we will be able to build healthy lives and healthy communities.

One of the greatest storehouses of treasure to examine is the collection of classical Christian writing that comes from the saints that have gone before us. As we go into the future we will need courage to follow the Holy Spirit into new and culturally relevant ways of thinking. However, there is a great deal from the past that we dare not lose. The writings of ancient Christians can help us to understand how they fought to remain faithful in the midst of the challenges that they faced, and they can inspire us to face our own. They are also filled with wisdom, though often it is necessary to forgive or discard some aspect of their thinking that we would not be able to accept today.

In this chapter I am going to present a thematic study that draws on Scripture, classical Christian writing, and contemporary experience to try to demonstrate how intimacy with God can be deepened by better thinking about God. As I do this, I am also trying to show that familiarity with the great writings of our Christian heritage can help us to improve these thoughts.

The theme is about bondage and it is about freedom. I call it "The Fat Soul Method of Breaking Free From Sins, Habits, and Addictions."

THE CROSS OF CHRIST

It begins like this: Thomas à Kempis (1380–1471) said in *The Imitation of Christ*, "Jesus has many who love His Kingdom in Heaven, but few who bear His Cross."[1]

He has correctly identified a problem. Many people love the benefits that Jesus has to bring, but not as many are eager to share His life of suffering and sacrifice. Thomas thinks that this is strange and goes on to list the benefits that come from "taking up" the Cross. The following passage may well be the most profound description of the Cross of Christ in all Christian literature:

> Why, then, do you fear to take up the Cross, which is the road to the Kingdom? In the Cross is salvation; in the Cross is life; in the Cross is protection against our enemies; in the Cross is infusion of heavenly sweetness; in the Cross is strength of mind; in the Cross is joy of spirit; in the Cross is excellence of virtue; in the Cross is perfection of holiness. There is no salvation of soul, nor hope of eternal life, save in the Cross. Take up the Cross, therefore, and follow Jesus, and go forward into eternal life. Christ has gone before you, bearing His Cross; He died for you on the Cross, that you also may bear your cross, and desire to die on the cross with Him. For if you die with Him, you will also live with Him. And if you share His sufferings, you will also share His glory.[2]

The Cross is here declared to be the path to freedom, but one is left wondering, "How does it work?" In fact, what we often find as we visit different communities of believers is that many have started on the path of spiritual growth hoping for great freedom in their lives. Unfortunately, as time has gone by their progress has slowed, leaving some in various stages of disappointment. I think I know the reason for this. Many Christians are trying to become perfect with very thin souls; they are not strong enough to make the changes they desire. In fact, each of us is desperately in need of a fattened soul.

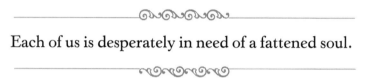

Each of us is desperately in need of a fattened soul.

This concept first came to me through an experience of church growth, but I was later delighted to find it in an important classical source—*The Confessions* by St. Augustine. First, let me describe the experience.

FATTENED SOUL

My wife and I planted a church in the fall of 1992 that met in a rural community hall for the first three years. Growth seemed painfully slow. One day a student of mine who attended the church told me that he had seen me in a dream the night before breaking into shops in our town. He tried to stop me, thinking it improper behavior for a pastor, but he said I kept right on. He also said that I seemed quite happy about it. I felt that this was actually a dream from God meant to encourage us that many people would soon start coming to our church. I told him that if this happened he should keep a pen and pad by his bed because he would know that God was speaking to him in his dreams.

The next Sunday our church grew spontaneously by 50 percent. People came from an hour away in three different directions without any knowledge of the others. Many were people we had worked with for a long time. Suddenly, they were ready to commit to being part of our church.

Less than a week later, a woman that I had not seen in years phoned me and told me that she had had a dream about Mary Ellen and me. In the dream we were both extremely fat. She woke up asking God why she was dreaming about people she no longer saw, and she asked about the fatness. In her mind, as an answer, she immediately heard the words of Proverbs: *"He that putteth his trust in the Lord shall be made fat"* (Prov. 28:25 KJV). Over the phone she said, "So I thought something good must have just happened to your church—has it?"

I marveled at this sequence of events, but I was also taken with the concept of fatness—whatever it was, it seemed like a good thing.

Later, when I was reviewing Augustine's *Confessions* for a class that I was going to teach, I came across this passage:

> Narrow is the mansion of my soul; enlarge Thou it, that Thou mayest enter in. It is ruinous! Repair Thou it. It has that within which must offend Thine eyes; I confess and know it. But who shall cleanse it? Or to whom should I cry, save Thee? Lord, cleanse me from my secret faults, and spare Thy servant from the power of the enemy.[3]

Augustine was crying out for a fattened soul! "Narrow is the mansion of my soul; enlarge Thou it, that Thou mayest enter in."

Apparently, those that trust the Lord are made fat, and souls that are fat make a better landing place for God's Presence.

This led, of course, to questions about why some souls remain thin. I decided that a key text might be in Galatians:

> But now that you have come to know God, **or rather to be known by God,** how is it that you turn back again to the weak and worthless elemental things, to which you desire to be enslaved all over again? (Galatians 4:9 NASB)

Perhaps it is possible to know God or, at least, to know something about Him or His power, without allowing Him to know us. This thought seemed strange at first—doesn't God know everything? Well, the answer may be closer to "no" than we think. Let me explain.

A good analogy has to do with God's omnipresence. This is the word we use to describe the reality that God is everywhere, in and through all that He has made (see Ps. 139; Jer. 23:23-24; Col. 1:16-17). And yet there are places where God is not, or perhaps it is better to say there are places where He is not in the same way as He is in other places. For instance, we are told that if we draw near to God, He will draw near to us (see James 4:8). Also, believers from the church at Laodicea (presumably along with the rest of us) are given the following invitation: "Behold, I stand at the door and knock; if anyone hears My voice and opens the door, I will come in to him and will dine with him, and he with Me" (Rev. 3:20 NASB). The God who is everywhere is not in the heart of the one who rejects Him in the same way as He is in the heart of people who welcome His Presence.

What about God's knowledge? We so easily say that God knows everything, and well we should (see Ps. 139; 1 John 3:20). However, there is a fascinating idea that emerges in the writing of Jeremiah that could make us question what this actually means. As God explains to Jeremiah that judgment is coming upon the people of Judah for their wicked ways—specifically, the practice of burning their children in sacrifice to the god, Moloch—He makes the following comment:

> *They have built the high places of Topheth, which is in the valley of the son of Hinnom,⁴ to burn their sons and their daughters in the fire, which I did not command, and it did not come into My mind* (Jeremiah 7:31 NASB).

If something did not come into God's mind, in a way we could say that He did not know it. This passage leaves us with the thought that humans may be capable of inventing or perpetrating evil that God would never have imagined. And, of course, this idea fits as well with the warning that Jesus gives in the Sermon on the Mount to those who did acts of power but kept their hearts protected from God's penetrating gaze: *"I never knew you; depart from Me..."* (Matt. 7:23 NASB).

Based on these thoughts, I think it may be far more important that we let God know us than that we know Him. Apparently people can even do miracles without inviting God deeply enough into their hearts to be known by Him or to be changed by Him.

People can even do miracles without inviting God deeply enough into their hearts to be known by Him or to be changed by Him.

This would be an example of resisting grace. And it would help to account for the sorry condition of some souls. Why is it that anyone

would want to keep God out of the depths of their being? Perhaps they are so afraid of being known and found wanting that they build large walls of pride to protect themselves even from love. Thomas à Kempis challenged us to find freedom in taking up the Cross. This may be what it will look like for some of us—making the painful decision to let God shine His Light on who or what we actually are, not on what we wish we were.

RESISTING GRACE

Almost a thousand years ago, Bernard of Clairvaux (1090–1153) wrote about how difficult this is to do, even in religious communities (and some would say, "Especially there!"):

> There are many ways of making excuses for sin. One person will say, "I did not do it." Another will say, "I did it but it was the right thing to do." Another will admit that it was wrong but say, "It was not very wrong." Another will concede that it was very wrong, but he will say, "I meant well." If he is forced to admit that he did not mean well, he will say as happened in the case of Adam and Eve, that someone else persuaded him to do it. If a man defends even his obvious sins in that way, when will he humbly confess to his abbot his hidden sins and the wicked thoughts which come into his heart?[5]

Contemporary psychiatrist, Gerald May, sees a similar reality in those who battle addictions. He lists the following elements of denial:

- Rationalization

- Hiding

- Delaying tactics

- "I can't handle it."

- "I can handle it."

- Breakdown

- Collusion (secret agreements)[6]

It seems as though some battles and some human responses have been constant for a long time.

Now, if resisting grace is an explanation for the thinness of some souls, it makes sense to ask how we could open ourselves to grace, to the penetrating Light that secures us, unmasks us, and finally changes us. How can we obtain a fat soul? I decided to study the word "fat" in the Old Testament to see if there were clues. As I began looking things up, my first impression was that the Hebrews had as many words for fat as Eskimos have for snow—apparently quite a few. Some of them represented concepts that were positive and some negative. The word that had been used in Proverbs 28:25 in the woman's dream about our church growth experience was *dashen,* and it was virtually always positive. It is translated differently in different versions, but it tends to mean one of the following: "to be fat," "to become fat," "to grow fat," "to prosper," or "to become prosperous."[7] I studied the references to this word in the Old Testament and was particularly impressed with the way it was used in the Psalms and in the Book of Proverbs.

I found it in Psalm 22, which I take ultimately to be a Messianic Psalm, in this verse: *"All the **prosperous** [dashen] of the earth will eat and worship, all those who go down to the dust will bow before Him, even he who cannot keep his soul alive"* (Ps. 22:29 NASB). It seems to indicate that the great ones of the earth—not in a pompous but in a real sense—will worship a living One who has died a cruel death that seems so much in line with Jesus' experience. I believe the first clue to acquiring a fat soul is to be "in Christ"—to become a worshiper of Jesus.

I found it next in Psalm 92. This passage stood out:

> *The righteous man will flourish like the palm tree, he will grow like a cedar in Lebanon. Planted in the house of the Lord, they will flourish in the courts of our God. They will still yield fruit in old age; they shall be **full of sap** [dashen] and very green, to declare that the Lord is upright; He is my rock, and there is no unrighteousness in Him* (Psalms 92:12-15 NASB).

Here was another clue—the kind of fat soul that continues to grow for a lifetime and to *"yield fruit in old age"* will most often be *"planted in the house of the Lord."* In other words, fat souls are more easily obtained by those who remain "in fellowship" with others who are also seeking God.

In Proverbs 11 there was another clue: *"The generous man will be **prosperous** [dashen], and he who waters will himself be watered"* (Prov. 11:25 NASB). Generosity plays a role. Hoarding keeps a soul small and impoverished. Those that open their hands to give place themselves in the stream of God's blessing and provision.

Those that open their hands to give place themselves in the stream of God's blessing and provision.

Next came Proverbs 13: *"The soul of the sluggard craves and gets nothing, but the soul of the diligent is* **made fat** *[dashen]"* (Prov. 13:4). Apparently, growth demands our best effort. We are called to participate with God, to partner with Him, in our spiritual formation.

Then there was Proverbs 15:30: *"Bright eyes gladden the heart; good news puts* **fat** *[dashen] on the bones"* (Prov. 15:30 NASB). It made sense. Both giving and receiving encouragement help to make a soul rich. Although it is clear that the quality of our speaking reveals a great deal about who we really are in the depths of our being, it is also true that the choices we make about speech patterns will have a lot to do with the kind of people we end up becoming.

All of these helped to form a picture of a growing soul. Those who are in Christ, in fellowship, and who are generous, diligent, and speak well, giving and receiving encouragement, are on their way to becoming fat souls. But one important passage remained, the original verse from the dream—*"An arrogant man stirs up strife, but he who trusts in the Lord will* **prosper** *[dashen]"* (Prov. 28:25 NASB).

In the end, I think that this idea is more important than some of the others. After we've done our best to be faithful and to hang in there, after we've tried our hardest and done our best, there is still a need for us to simply trust. More important than our own effort in the growth process is the love of God that knows us and changes us. We cannot do it without Him. The great key to becoming a fat soul is this—trusting that God is with us, improving the condition of our souls as we keep abiding in Him, even if we are not yet who we want to be.

LOVED IN OUR IMPERFECTION

Probably no one has said this better than Thérèse de Lisieux (1873–1897)—a French Carmelite nun who died early of tuberculosis—in a letter to one of her sisters: "If you are willing to serenely bear the trial of being displeasing to yourself, then you will be for Jesus a pleasant place of shelter."[8] What an insight! It seems to be part of the human condition to be "displeasing to yourself." Almost everyone understands this. And the consequence of an embarrassment at our own imperfection can keep us from jumping wholeheartedly into life. It can also tempt us to keep others, and God, at arm's length. Thérèse realized that if we can get over this displeasure, if we can "serenely bear" this trial, we will be a very peaceful place for Jesus to come. We will provide for Him a "pleasant place of shelter."

Many people are unconsciously waiting to be perfect before they will allow God to come close to them. They don't understand that this is a position of pride that will keep God from a great deal of their experience. It will also make sure that their souls remain thin. If, instead, they could accept that God's love is so great that He accepts them as they are, they would be able to welcome Him into their lives in a way that would transform them forever.

I have a friend who was secretly bulimic for many years. She hated herself. In her own way she loved God, but she was tentative and broken as a person due to the many hard circumstances of her life. After she joined our church and received a great deal of love and attention and was prayed for many times, she had an encounter with Jesus that greatly enhanced her healing process. In fact, from this moment she began to have accurate understanding of what others were going through and was able, often, to speak into their lives as though God

Himself was speaking through her. Her ability astonished and comforted people in their distress.

But she continued to hate herself. One night, around midnight, she called our home and wailed her anguish into the phone. I was exhausted and I thought, "God, You have to help me because I can't go up to her apartment and bring her back here—I'm too tired. Help!" As she kept screaming and crying, a single word popped into my mind. I didn't know what else to do, but I realized that God's strength is sometimes best revealed in our weakness, and I decided to take a chance that the word was from Him. It was probably one of the least responsible decisions I have made as a pastor. I said, "Stop crying. I have a word for you from God."

> If, instead, they could accept that God's love is so great that He accepts them as they are, they would be able to welcome Him into their lives in a way that would transform them forever.

She had great trust in Mary Ellen and me, and also several others from our community who had spent a good deal of time with her. She did stop crying, and she asked, "What is it?"

I offered up the word; it was all I had. "Tricycle," I said, feeling foolish.

She roared back into screaming. Then, a moment later, she stopped and she challenged me. "Why?" she demanded.

Suddenly I knew; I can't say how. "Well," I explained, "when someone is riding a tricycle they have an extra wheel that gives them balance and stability until they're able to ride a bicycle. In your case, God has given you a true spiritual gift to help others, even though you are not yet healed yourself. His love, which is with you now, is your third wheel. It's His way of showing you that He loves you as you are. And it means that it won't be long until you will be riding a bicycle with the best of them."

Her crying stopped. Quietly, she said, "I left the home where I was abused and beaten for 23 years the day after I had a dream that I was riding a broken bicycle."

In the years that followed, this person became one of the joys of our community as she matured and became a leader in caring for others. One of our pastors, a gifted counselor and family therapist, said, "Never before have I seen one person helped by so many, turn around and become the one who gives help to so many others." All of this happened because of trust.

This is why I believe that having a fat soul makes all the difference. The thin soul cannot change by itself. If it chooses to remain thin by refusing to let God come near, it is caught in the consequence of an impoverished life, often held back by many fears and points of bondage. If, on the other hand, a soul welcomes God into its life in an honest way, even if it is extremely broken, it will begin to change. As it gets richer and stronger, many sins and habits and addictions will simply fall away.

In fact, as we trust that God is with us, loves us, wants us to improve, as we keep coming back to Him, as we accept our sin and our addictions, as we tell others without shame, as we ask for help, as we struggle forward, as we abide in Him, our souls will get fatter and fatter—there will come a day when our greatest struggles will not be enough to restrain the "breaking forward" of our souls.

I hope you've enjoyed this thematic study based on Scripture, classical Christian writing, and contemporary experience. I would be pleased if it helped you to desire to grow in familiarity with Scripture and long for more intimate experiences with God for yourself. I also hope that it will help to inspire a taste for reading some of the great treasury of classical literature that is part of the heritage of the Christian Church. Most of all, I hope that it helps you to become a fat soul!

ENDNOTES

1. Thomas à Kempis, *The Imitation of Christ*, trans. Leo Sherley-Price (London, UK: Penguin Books, 1952), 83.

2. Ibid., 84-85.

3. Augustine of Hippo, *The Confessions*, trans. E.B. Pusey, vol. 18 of Great Books of the Western World, eds. Robert M. Hutchins and Mortimer J. Adler (Chicago, IL: Encyclopedia Britannica, 1952), 2.

4. A derivative name, Gehenna, is Jesus' normal way to speak of hell. This valley of Hinnom, south of Jerusalem, with a history of child sacrifice and the burning of refuse, made an excellent picture for His listeners.

5. Bernard of Clairvaux, "On Humility and Pride," from Bernard of Clairvaux: Selected Works, trans. G.R. Evans, The Classics of Western Spirituality (New York, NY: Paulist Press, 1987), 135.

6. Gerald G. May, *Addiction and Grace* (San Francisco, CA: Harper and Row, 1988), 42-52.

7. James Strong, *Strong's Exhaustive Concordance of the Bible* (Peabody, MA: Hendrickson Publishers, first published in 1894), ISBN 0-917006-01-1, 1878.

8. Thérèse de Lisieux, *Collected Letters of Thérèse de Lisieux*, trans. F. J. Sheed (New York: Sheed and Ward, 1949), 303.

CHAPTER 10

Servants and Slaves and Sons

STEVE LONG

I'm a son. I'm the oldest of six children born to Charles and Mary Long. I was born during my parent's year-long honeymoon and just before they went back to Malawi, Africa, where they served as missionaries.

My dad and mom met in Malawi while each was on their first term. My father was based in the very south of the nation. Part of his role was to travel to the various villages where there were churches and train the pastors who could not afford to attend Bible school.

My mom was serving in the middle of the nation along with one other gal from her church in London, England. As my mother tells it, my father arrived unannounced one day to visit the local pastor.

He was told that there were two white women in the village. When my parents met, they just knew they were to marry. Not love at first; rather, they just knew that this was the person they were to marry.

So, my father from Toronto and my mother from London spent their honeymoon year in England and Canada. My parents did fall in love and during the year got to know each other's family members and tour a bit of the two nations.

I was born in Toronto, and three months later my parents were back in Malawi, where they started a Bible school, which is still functioning today. Eighteen months later, my brother Richard was born, and another eighteen months later, Jennifer was born.

I'm sure that my parents were very proud to have a son. I know that they loved me—but! The "but" in my life was a lie I believed that hindered my relationships with God, my parents, my siblings, my wife, my two sons, my colleagues, my church, everything.

Want to know what the lie was? Well, you'll have to wait until I tell you the story of two sons who also believed lies.

One of the best known stories in the Bible is from Luke 15 where Jesus tells us about a father and his two sons. The story begins this way:

> *There was a man who had two sons. The younger one said to his father, "Father, give me my share of the estate." So he divided his property between them* (Luke 15:11-12).

Each son was given a portion of the estate. If Jewish custom was followed in the story, the older son would be given a double share. It appears that the older son was given the farm while the younger son was given a large amount of cash.

The story goes on to say that while the money was there, so were the friends. While the money was there, so were the parties and the lifestyle that goes with wild living.

The money is soon gone. So are the friends, and now the country where he lives is in recession. The only job this young Jewish boy can find is to work on a pig farm. The shame and reproach go farther than working with pigs. While he does have a job, his salary is not in money but in food—pigs' food.

One day, as Jesus tells the story, the son comes to his senses and has a revelation. The revelation is this—even the servants, the men and women hired to work on his dad's farm, get better treatment than this!

He makes up his mind that humbling himself and going back to his dad would be better than working with pigs. At his father's farm the servants get a salary, not pig food.

The day comes and he begins the journey home. As he goes he thinks through his past, and without realizing it, a lie from satan slips in and contaminates the truth. The lie so negatively affects the truth that if it were not for the father recognizing the lie and rebuking it, the son would have missed his destiny!

What was the lie? It is one that most of us carry into our relationships, especially our relationship with God. It is so damaging that we can miss the very intimacy with God that He so much wants us to receive!

THE LIE: MY PAST MAKES ME UNWORTHY TO BE A SON

This son of a wealthy farmer now believes that the best he can hope for is to be a servant, one of his dad's hired men. Listen as he talks to himself.

I will set out and go back to my father and say to him: Father,
I have sinned against Heaven and against you. I am no longer
worthy to be called your son; make me like one of your hired
men (Luke 15:18-19).

This lie—that his past somehow affects his relationship with his father—is very common. His thinking process goes something like this:

"I sinned against my father by wasting all my inheritance. He
won't like that!

"I sinned against God by living a reckless lifestyle. I had sex with
women I wasn't married to, I got drunk, and I also broke the law of
God and worked with pigs. God won't like that!

"I'm therefore unworthy to be a son. I'm unworthy to be my dad's
son and I'm unworthy to be a son of God. My past has caught up to me
and I'm now paying the price. My relationship with God and my dad
can never be the same again. I'm unworthy!"

Sound familiar? Almost every single person on planet earth has
felt this way. Most of us have believed this lie, and because we didn't
know it was a lie it has become truth to us!

What is the truth? Well it just so happens that this particular dad
represents our Father in Heaven perfectly. That being the case, the
father in the story immediately picks up on the lie and challenges it
head on.

But the father said to his servants, "Quick! Bring the best robe
and put it on him. Put a ring on his finger and sandals on his
feet. Bring the fattened calf and kill it. Let's have a feast and
celebrate. For this son of mine was dead and is alive again;

he was lost and is found." So they began to celebrate (Luke 15:22-24).

The Truth: Sons Are Always Sons—They Occasionally Get Lost

What a father! His first thought is a "but." The Father will hear nothing of the lie and puts into motion a series of acts that brings immediate restoration. The father's orders to the servants overrode the lie of unworthiness. His words beautifully established the boy, who thought he was a servant, as his son! Sons are always sons!

We often face the very same challenge as this young man. Things have happened to us in our past, circumstances came about and stuff happened that we now wish didn't happen. Can we change the past? Rarely. Does our past have to be our future? No! Can we change what we believe about the situation? Absolutely!

This son believed that his relationship with his natural dad would be tainted forever. He also believed that the strict God that he had abandoned wouldn't want him back, either.

If we get the revelation of what our Father in Heaven is really like and accept His truth into our lives, we'll remain as sons.

Do our negative past experiences affect God and other relationships today? Every time! Especially if we, too, believe the lie that we are unworthy. But if we get the revelation of what our Father in Heaven is really like and accept His truth into our lives, we'll remain as sons.

By the way, ladies, you are a son whether you like it or not! In the Old Testament, women didn't get an inheritance, only the men. The good news is that with a relationship with Jesus, *"There is neither Jew nor Greek, slave nor free, male nor female, for you are all one in Christ Jesus"* (Gal. 3:28).

Guys, if you are thinking you're exempt from a new mind-set, sorry. We have to get our heads around being the "Bride of Christ." God likes taking everyone out of their boxes and putting us in a privileged place!

So the question now needs to be asked—do you see yourself before God as a favored son, or do you see yourself as an unworthy servant? Servants serve. Servants work hard for the master. Servants at best get a fair reward at the end of the day. Servants don't get the intimate relationship that sons do.

In your heart, what do you feel right now? Son or servant? If you responded by saying that you have servant tendencies, I have good news for you. Later, I'm going to lead you through some prayers that will reestablish you as a worthy son! Did you remember that this story had two sons? Let's talk about the older son now. Did you know that he also believed a lie? His lie was just as damaging and it, too, was meant by satan to rob him of his destiny.

As the story continues in Luke 15, the older son is out in the fields and hears the party happening back at the ranch house. He inquires of a servant what is going on and hears about his brother's return. His response is anger.

Imagine the pain of the father on hearing that his older son won't join them on this special day. Just as the father had run to redeem the younger son, the father ran out a second time in one day to find the older brother and bring him home. When the father and older son meet, the son vents angrily. His words betray that he has already believed a lie. Somehow, satan has also influenced this older son.

Did you know that out of your mouth comes what your heart believes? That is good and bad news. The good news is that if we have friends who have ears to hear, they can catch the lies just like this amazing father did.

Did you know that you can also train yourself to catch lies? As we seek after intimacy with the Father, we will slowly begin to hear our own words and recognize that something isn't right. Listen to the older son and see if you can hear his lie.

Look! All these years I've been slaving for you and never disobeyed your orders. Yet you never gave me even a young goat so I could celebrate with my friends. But when this son of yours who has squandered your property with prostitutes comes home, you kill the fattened calf for him! (Luke 15:29-30)

Did you hear it? Did you hear *"this son of yours"*? He has mentally and emotionally distanced himself from both his brother and father. But that isn't the big one. The big lie is found in his first sentence when he says, *"I've been slaving for you."* Do you see what he believes? He doesn't see himself as a son but as a slave!

The Lie: I Have to Perform for Love

Look again:

All these years I've been slaving for you and never disobeyed your orders. You never gave me even a young goat so I could celebrate with my friends (Luke 15:29).

Several small lies contribute to the big lie. This older son in his heart believes he has gone from being a son to a slave. He also believes that one qualifies to be a son by obeying orders. Sadly, he also believes that his father was never generous with him nor allowed him to have parties.

A slave is a large step down the scale from a servant. Servants have rights in most cultures—they at least get a salary. Slaves have no rights and get nothing. They are property!

This older son, deep in his heart, believes that nothing he has ever done for his father matters. Mentally, he has positioned himself as a slave—a worthless being, who never will receive any affection or any reward! This lie has also changed his relationship with his father to one of orders and obedience. If he obeys he gets approval, if he disobeys he gets discipline.

Many of us have grown up with this subtle lie embedded in us. Almost all parents reward good behavior and discipline bad behavior. In our formative years, we heard "good girl" and "bad boy" associated with what we did.

Many of us have grown up with this subtle lie embedded in us. In our formative years, we heard "good girl" and "bad boy" associated with what we did.

The third part of this lie is the statement that his father never even gave him a young goat. Lies are so insidious that they absolutely distort the truth. Do you remember the very first verse of this story? The story began with:

There was a man who had two sons. The younger one said to his father, "Father, give me my share of the estate." So he divided his property between them (Luke 15:11-12).

What was the inheritance of the older son? It would appear that a full division of assets took place and the older son was given the farm!

This lie is so mean, so crippling, and so damaging that the older son has lost sight that he now owns the farm! He is still working for his father's approval, even though the father has no more assets to give away! Not only does this son own all the goats, he also owns the farm! Satan has robbed this older son of the farm that his loving father gave him! Listen as the father speaks the truth:

"My son," the father said, "you are always with me, and everything I have is yours" (Luke 15:31).

THE TRUTH: SONS ARE ALWAYS SONS—THEY OCCASIONALLY GET CONFUSED

The lie that many of us have to deal with is whether God accepts us just for who we are. Do I need to work for His love and approval, just like I had to for my parents to love me? Does God love me more if I'm the first one to church meetings, if I stay the longest, volunteer the most, sacrifice the most, give the most, complain the least?

All these traits are that of an orphan—someone without a father. Sadly, this older son was so confused by the lies his heart believed that he no longer had a dad nor a brother. Confusion reigned in his life! In his own mind he had ceased being a son and now was a slave. He had to do the right things, work the hardest, and try hard to be noticed. Classic orphan-spirit beliefs.

Did you know that most of us view Father God like one of these two sons? The disciples, after three years of being with Jesus, were still servants and slaves. It would appear that none of them knew the Father like Jesus knew the Father. Jesus' promise was that he would *"not leave* [them] *as orphans"* (John 14:18). He wanted each of his men to be a son!

Whole cultures have difficulty seeing God as Father, let alone a loving Father. Did you know that in the Old Testament God is only called "Father" three times? God was not seen as close, cuddly, and on a first-name basis by the nation of Israel. Did you also know that God sent His Son to clarify the issue and bring truth regarding who He is? Jesus called God "Father" about 300 times! Wow, talk about a change of mind-set.

No wonder the disciples had no clue who the Father was! They were speaking a different language than Jesus was regarding the Father. They were thinking like servants and slaves rather than being sons!

Let's go back to my story now. Remember, I'm the firstborn son of missionary parents in Malawi, Africa. I know that my parents love me—but! So, what's the "but"?

The "but" is a lie that came to me from satan when I was about one year old. I've seen this scenario several times as I've had people minister to me. I know it well!

I'm in my bedroom and it's bedtime. The door in my room is a glass paneled one so I can see through into the eating area of our home where my parents were entertaining some of the African leaders.

I don't know why, but I want one of my parents to come and cuddle with me. I may have needed my diaper changed or was still hungry, I don't know. I can see myself standing up in my crib and calling for my parents.

My parents don't come. I cry out louder. Still no response, so I shake the sides of the crib and yell for my parents. Neither of them seems to notice me, and therefore neither one comes.

I've rationalized this out many times. I can see my parents enjoying their company. They are laughing and either don't hear me or have made the choice not to respond.

For those of you under the age of 45, let me give you some history into child-rearing in the 1950s. The premise was this—kids are to be seen and not heard. Let them cry themselves to sleep, don't give them too much love or attention as it will spoil them.

I've already mentioned that my mom is English. What I didn't tell you was that, while my father was from Toronto, his parents were raised in Scotland. Neither the Scots nor the Brits are known for their extravagant, emotional, expressive love! So I grew up not receiving hugs. I don't remembering hearing the words "I love you," although I'm sure they were spoken. Love seemed to be conditional on my good behavior.

What was whispered in my ear was this: "Your parents don't love you. They've abandoned you emotionally."

While I was in my crib, waiting for my parents to come, satan visited me. Not in person, but via a thought—a lie. What was whispered in my ear was this: "Your parents don't love you. They've abandoned you emotionally."

As a one-year-old, the circumstances seemed to match the lie. My parents chose not to come to pick me up. They preferred the company of others. They had a nanny that looked after me so that they could devote their full time to the Bible school. I was abandoned!

Did my parents reject me? No! My parents made many large sacrifices for my siblings and me. I know that now, but as a child growing up I felt that I wasn't loved or appreciated. To complicate things, my brother Richard and sister Jennifer were born while we were living in Africa. When I was five my parents took a year off, visiting England and then Canada. As it turned out, my parents felt the call of God to stay in Canada, and my dad became the pastor of a Baptist church.

Three other siblings were born, and now we were a family with six kids. As with most large families, the attention of the parents was divided. It became obvious to me that I wasn't the favorite of either of my parents.

So what do you do to get attention from people you are desperate to have love you? Sports will do it! The only problem was my brother Richard seemed to be more of an athlete than me. He got the attention.

Academics will do it! Well, another problem—both Richard and Jennifer were accelerated. In fact, Richard, though he was 18 months younger than I, caught up to me in school by doing second grade in the mornings and third grade, where I was, in the afternoons. They got the attention.

Good behavior will do it! Well that would be impossible. My sister Jennifer was evil and neither of my parents could see it. (That was my impression at the time—Jennifer is not evil!) They thought everything she did was perfect. She got the attention.

I'll be likeable! Once again, a problem. My youngest siblings, Brian and Liz, were as cute as buttons, and everything they did got them attention.

Ah, but there were other ways to get noticed! I became the clown, and when that didn't work I became rebellious. Even rebel kids get attention. Not for the right reasons, but they do get attention! Still a problem. My middle sister Trish was more rebellious than me! (She's since tamed down and attends our church.)

So how does this relate to my adult years? Fast-forward to when I'm in my thirties. I'm married with two young sons and an amazing wife, Sandra. I'm a Baptist pastor. I'm also still living in the lie that love is earned; love is conditional.

At one of the churches we helped pastor, I was hired specifically to increase the attendance of the church. Finally, a place where I can be loved based on measurable goals! If I can grow the church, I'll be accepted!

The church did grow. I got my financial bonus in half the time the board had expected. But, there is still a love deficit. I know—I'll get my peers to accept and acknowledge me.

Not knowing that I was being driven by lies, our church began to live on the edge. We were the first church in our denomination to have a worship band. We were the first church to let the pastors wear jeans. We were the first church in our network to do "seeker-targeted" church meetings. We had dramas, we had slick marketing, and we got noticed. I was now writing regular articles for our denominational magazine. I was invited to serve on denominational boards.

Without realizing what I was doing, I was using our church family as a tool for my love needs. I didn't intentionally think this up, it just happened; it just became a way of life.

Sandra was trying to reach out to me with unconditional love, but by now I didn't know what that was. I would come home from the church office just after 5 P.M., and within minutes of getting in our house, I would lose my temper with our preschool boys. The house isn't clean enough, the food isn't cooked right, and nothing is good enough! I didn't know it, but I had literally become an older son! I was an orphan and striving for love!

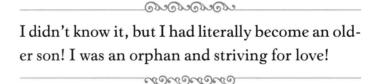

I didn't know it, but I had literally become an older son! I was an orphan and striving for love!

But then! The Bible teaches that, *"We love because he first loved us"* (1 John 4:19). God's unconditional, extravagant, faithful love began to find me!

Perhaps a better way to say it is that I began to *let* God's unconditional, extravagant, faithful love find me. The "but" for me was a revival that began in Toronto at a church pastored by John and Carol Arnott.

It "just happened" that I met John and Carol in 1992. I was recommended to them by friends as a good conference planner. I helped organize a couple of conferences for their church in 1993 and was even asked to join their church. The timing just wasn't right for us to join Toronto Airport Christian Fellowship (TACF). In January 1994, God visited this church and a worldwide revival began.

Sandra and I were invited by John and Carol to the first extended meeting where Randy Clark, a Vineyard pastor from St. Louis, Missouri, was speaking. We attended and had our very first experience with the Holy Spirit. Wow! What do you say after being on the floor for 20 minutes and experiencing God for the first time? What I felt was peace, but it actually was a huge dose of Father's love for me.

Within ten days of the revival starting, my Baptist church had loaned me to TACF and I found myself helping John and Carol organize the "Toronto Blessing." Within six months, I had joined the pastoral staff. Lots of attention!

I was way behind the rest of the pastors and prayer team in terms of the Spirit, and so at the beginning I just stood on the prayer lines and received. Slowly, I built up enough confidence to pray and minister to others. The primary revelation that God released in this revival was the Father's love. It seemed that everyone was becoming an expert at teaching on the Father's love. Except me.

As the revival moved on, my role was to attend three of the six nightly meetings and bridge the worship team and speaker. I heard over 100 sermons a year for about eight years in a row.

Of the thousand sermons I heard, at least a quarter of them were about the Father's love. Many of them were preached just for me! Specialists such as Jack Winter, Peter and Heather Jackson, Ed and Janet Piorek, Jack and Trish Frost, and James and Denise Jordan regularly spoke on the unconditional, extravagant, faithful love of Father God.

As God's love came my way, I began to see things better. I recognized lies that I had believed. I saw walls that kept love from coming my way and kept me from loving others. The first time I saw the picture of me as a child in the crib was when Will and Madeline Walker ministered to me. They were a part of our pastoral team and knew my parents from Africa days! They were our in-house specialists, and if we were having "emotional" problems we'd go to them. Needless to say, I rarely sought them out for personal ministry. I didn't have problems, others did!

An issue arose in my life, and in the course of needing ministry, Will and Madeline identified rejection and abandonment issues. When they asked Father God to show me the root, this picture came. For the first time in my life I had a memory to go with the pain I was feeling. They led me through a number of repentance prayers for vows, judgments, and soul spirit hurts. I felt a great release of pain as they prayed. That memory would come to me often and I would pray deeper into the various aspects of my lie. That memory of me in the crib was now not a threatening, hurtful place, but one of peace.

Last year I was in that memory again, and the Lord spoke to me of another lie. This one I had not heard before. The Father spoke to me and said something like: "You've been blaming your parents for years for not loving you; that isn't the truth."

What! I asked the Father to clarify this and what He said shocked me so much that I left what I was doing and drove 30 minutes across our city to get verification face to face from my mom. (My dad had died a number of years ago so I couldn't check with him.) What the Father said to me was that the reason why my parents didn't hug me was that I had closed my heart to them, not the other way around! This was a bombshell to me! It was about 8 P.M. when this revelation came.

My mother suffered a stroke a couple years ago and has had to move out of her apartment into a care facility. Her normal bedtime is 9 P.M., so when I arrived at 8:45 P.M. she was already in bed and about to turn the lights out. I told her about the memory I had as a one-year-old and how in my mind over the past years the issue was her and Dad's lack of love to me. I explained to her that the new insight the Father had given me was that I was to blame and not them.

I asked her straight out: "Did I let you hug me and pick me up as a child?"

My mother laughed. Laughing isn't a good sign when you are looking for deep answers to life's hardest questions. She looked at me and said, "*No!* You never liked to be cuddled or picked up; you always wanted to be alone."

Ouch! I now had another set of prayers—repenting and confessing my sins to the Father.

As a pastor I hear both men and women share with me that their relationship with God is distant. They can't seem to engage like they feel others can. I know exactly where they are at. I've lived there. I have the T-shirt; in fact, I made the T-shirts!

For me, intimacy with the Father has been a long journey. I was 50 years of age when that last revelation came to me. I've been a full-time pastor since 1981 and a pastor at TACF since 1994.

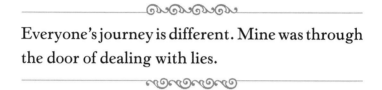

Everyone's journey is different. Mine was through the door of dealing with lies.

Everyone's journey is different. Mine was through the door of dealing with lies. If your journey is similar to mine, I'd like, as promised, to guide you through some ministry now. But first, let me remind you of truth from your Father!

I will be a Father to you, and you will be My sons and daughters, says the Lord Almighty (2 Corinthians 6:18).

The Father's agenda for you is that you will know Him as Father and will know that you are a son or daughter!

But when the time had fully come, God sent His Son, born of a woman, born under law, to redeem those under law, that we might receive the full rights of sons (Galatians 4:4-5).

The Father's desire for you is that you function in the fullness of a son just like Jesus did. In fact, one of the reasons Jesus died was to bring you to the Father! As Paul mentions in Romans 8, there is nothing that can separate me from the Father's love. You are never alone, never!

If you have identified with my story in any way, I'd like you to pray this prayer with me.

Father, would You reveal Yourself to me? Will You help me to see the areas in my past that have incorrectly clouded my view of who You are? I know You are my Father, but I need to know it in my heart, my emotions, and not just in my head.

Ask this question of the Father. After you ask the question, listen and hear what He says to you and write it down. Remember that His sheep hear His voice (see John 10:27). If you are more visual, you may see a picture like my memory as a child in the crib. Here's the question.

Father, what lie has kept me from receiving Your love in that memory?

_____

_____

_____

_____

_____

_____

Ask this question.

Father, what is the truth in that situation?

_____

_____

_____

Ask Jesus to now reveal Himself to you in that situation. The truth is that He is always with us even when we don't see Him. Close your eyes and sense where He is and what He is saying to you or doing for you.

_____

_____

_____

_____

If there are people that you now need to forgive, if there are vows that you've recognized or judgments you know you made, now is a good time to repent, renounce, forgive, and bless.

Father, I forgive _____ *(their name) for* _____ *(what they did or said). I repent of my response of* _____ *(what did you do?). I bless* _____ *(their name) today, in Jesus' Name.*

One last thing. It would appear from my reading of John 14:16-21 that one of the roles of the Holy Spirit is to bring the Father's love to you and me. Jesus, when talking to His men the night before His death, talked about a special day.

On that day you will realize that I am in My Father, and you are in Me, and I am in you (John 14:20).

I believe that is a direct reference to the experiences they would have in John 20 and Acts 2 when they received the Holy Spirit. Being with Jesus for three years hadn't altered the disciples much in terms of understanding the love of God. But a couple impact sessions with the Holy Spirit sure did!

You and I also need to keep getting full of the Holy Spirit. I'm convinced that He is the agent of Father God to bring His love to you and me. If you close the Holy Spirit off, you close off His love for you!

Normally, I'd get you to close your eyes while I pray this, but since you have to read the prayer, close your eyes as soon as you finish it and linger in His presence.

Holy Spirit, if one of Your roles is to bring the Father's love, please come and visit me now! Holy Spirit, fill me with my Father's love.

Let His love find you today! I know that if you say this prayer every day for a month, you'll become a son! I'm a son!

CHAPTER 11

Intimacy

DAVID RAVENHILL

Unfortunately, the first thought to enter our minds when we hear the word intimacy is to associate it with the physical and sexual realm. This is largely due to living in a sexually saturated, hedonistic society where our minds tend to gravitate to the temporal, physical pleasures rather than the eternal realm of the Spirit. This is especially true of the younger generation, who have a tendency to overdose on sensuality rather than spirituality. Because of this, we need to proceed with a certain caution when talking about intimacy, lest we overstep the bounds of biblical understanding and revelation.

In his 1828 edition of the *American Dictionary of the English Language*, Noah Webster defines "intimacy" as, "close friendship, fellowship, nearness in friendship, near, close, familiar, one whom the thoughts of another are entrusted without reserve, to share together, to love entirely."

What is so interesting about Webster's definition is the fact that he never relates intimacy with the sexual realm at all. I emphasize this, · because today in the Church we have so many choruses with lyrics about kissing and dancing, which tend to imply that our relationship with the Lord is largely of a physical nature only. As I pastor, I have had to counsel many young people who have been deceived by evil spirits, believing they were experiencing some type of sexual intimacy with the Lord. While the term *intimacy* does iply that of a deep personal relationship, we need to guard against using it in a purely physical or sexual way. God is a spirit and although Jesus was manifest in a human body the Scriptures tell us, *"He had no beauty...that we should desire Him"* (Isa. 53:2). We are not attracted to Jesus because of His "good looks," but rather His attributes, character, nature, and glory. Another danger associated with the term *intimacy* is to view it as something strictly romantic or mystical, thereby making it more of an emotional relationship than a volitional relationship.

Since I am writing only one chapter, I don't intend to use it to develop this any further, but did feel the need to raise this cautionary flag. To avoid any further misunderstanding of the term *intimacy*, I will replace it with the word *friendship*, which has a more scriptural basis. Jesus said to His disciples, *"No longer do I call you servants... but I have called you friends"* (John 15:15 NKJV). According to God's Word, a friend *"sticks closer than a brother"* (Prov. 18:24). We are also told, *"A friend loves at all times"* (Prov. 17:17). Everyone craves the companionship of a true friend, even God Himself. Abraham is referred to as *"the friend of God"* (James 2:23 NKJV). What is implied in true friendship?

TIME

Friendships normally form over time. People are drawn together as they become more and better acquainted with each other. Jesus appointed twelve disciples *"...that they might be with Him and that He might send them out to preach"* (Mark 3:14). Since the essence of good preaching is to make Christ known, the disciples had to spend time with Him in order to know Him. Once they knew Him they could tell others about Him. The longer we spend time with someone the more we understand them and learn their ways.

After Jesus had been taken up into Heaven, John wrote: *"... what we have heard, what we have seen with our eyes, what we have looked at and touched with our hands, concerning the Word of Life... we proclaim to you"* (1 John 1:1,3 NASB). The disciples came to know Him by spending time with Him and were therefore able to accurately reveal Him to others. The only way to know God is to spend time with Him. He reveals Himself to us through His Word. Any "revelation" that is in discord with His Word is not biblical revelation (see Isa. 8:19-20).

SIMILAR LIKES AND VALUES

Friendships form from having similar values and interests. We often hear expressions such as, "This is my golfing buddy or hunting partner," implying that they share a common interest. We have a beautiful picture of this in the first chapter of Song of Solomon. After falling head over heals in love with her beloved, the bride asks the bridegroom the question, "Where do you pasture your flock?" This former vine dresser suddenly becomes interested in knowing about sheep, the interest of her beloved shepherd. She understands the importance of having a common interest with her beloved if they are going to be united together in marriage. We read in the Scriptures, *"Can two walk together, unless they are agreed?"* (Amos 3:3 NKJV) Anyone who claims to have fellowship with God and yet fails to take an interest in the things that God is interested in is simply deceived. I heard A.W. Tozer say that the Christian life can be reduced down to this simple equation: "Learn to love what God loves and hate what God hates." This is the very essence of true friendship.

The first human relationship mentioned in the Scripture is that of Adam and Eve. After God had created Adam, He said, *"It is not good for the man to be alone"* (Gen. 2:18). God's intention for giving Eve to Adam was for companionship and friendship and also as a helper. Together they were called to fulfill their God-given purpose.

One day we will forever be united to the King of Kings; therefore, we need to understand what it means to reign with Him now.

In the same way, the Bride of Christ is given to Christ as a "helper." We are laborers together with Him. After we fall in love with Him, we fall in love with His passions, desires, and purpose. One day we will forever be united to the King of kings; therefore, we need to understand what it means to reign with Him now. We will be united to the Great Shepherd of the sheep; therefore, we need to ask God to place in us His love for the flock. We will marry the Great Physician, so we need to learn to bind up one another's wounds. We will likewise marry the Captain of the Hosts, so we had better learn how to fight.

We will also be united to the Judge of all the earth, so we had better learn how to pass righteous judgment. All of these things are necessary if we are to become His Bride and helper.

Abraham was referred to as God's friend because he was willing to cast in his lot with God and walk in obedience to everything God revealed to him. A study of Abraham's life will reveal that his relationship with God was not merely an emotional or mystical one, but a volitional one. Abraham had to overcome his deep emotions when making the difficult decision to leave family, friends, and farm and then harder yet, when God asked him to give up his son, Isaac, as a sacrifice. If Abraham's relationship with God had been purely sentimental he would have never followed through on God's demands, but rather yielded to his feelings. As I remember someone wisely saying, "Feelings are like a caboose; they follow the train, but it is our will that can be compared to the engine because that powers the train." There is nothing wrong with having emotions, provided they don't determine our obedience or lack thereof.

INVOLVEMENT

Friendships are formed when working together. While we have already touched on this in the previous segment, allow me to address it again. Jesus, when confronted by the multitudes who said to Him, *"Behold, Your mother and Your brothers are standing outside seeking to speak to You,"* replied by turning to those with Him and saying, *"Behold, My mother and My brothers! For whoever does the will of My Father who is in Heaven, he is My brother and sister and mother"* (Matt. 12:47,49-50 NASB). Jesus was saying, in essence, that the one who is involved in doing the will of God is really as close or closer to

Him than family. When Jesus referred to his disciples as "friends," He placed it in the context of *doing*. Notice what He told them: *"You are my friends **if you do** what I command"* (John 15:14).

While the Scriptures abound with admonitions about involvement, we need to guard against our involvement becoming the dominant issue in a relationship. While there is nothing wrong with becoming involved in God's purposes, we can easily become "purpose-driven" rather than "presence-driven." I carry in my Bible a page from a daily devotional calendar with the following quote from *A Touch of His Freedom* by Dr. Charles Stanley.

> I believe with all my heart that it is impossible to be both goal-oriented and God oriented at the same time. One orientation will always take precedence over the other. When our desire to achieve takes the lead, several things happen in our relationship with God. He becomes the means to an end rather than the end. We tend to use God rather than worship Him. We will find ourselves seeking *information about* Him rather than *transformation by* Him.[1]

OBEDIENCE

It is impossible to have a relationship with God and walk in disobedience to His Word. Listen to what John writes in his first epistle.

> *The one who says, "I have come to know Him" and does not keep His commandments, is a liar, and the truth is not in him* (1 John 2:4 NASB).

Jesus said, *"If you love me, you will keep my commandments"* (John 14:15 NASB). Love is not some sentimental feeling of well-being, but rather, that purposeful commitment to walk in obedience to the will of God as revealed to us through His Word. We are told that *"God demonstrates His own love toward us, in that while we were yet sinners, Christ died for us"* (Rom. 5:8 NASB). We likewise should *demonstrate* our love for Him by walking in obedience to His Word.

OTHERS

The Bible emphatically declares that it is impossible to love God and yet not love your brother. *"The one who does not love does not know God, for God is love"* (1 John 4:8 NASB). Jesus put it far more graphically when He said:

> *I was hungry, and you gave Me nothing to eat; I was thirsty, and you gave Me nothing to drink; I was a stranger, and you did not invite Me in; naked, and you did not clothe Me; sick, and in prison, and you did not visit Me* (Matthew 25:42-43 NASB).

Those listening were shocked, asking, "When did we see You with all these needs?" To which Jesus responds. *"...to the extent that you did not do it to one of the least of these, you did not do it to Me"* (Matt. 25:45 NASB). The measure to which we love God's people is the measure to which we love God. No more and no less.

Love is not some sentimental feeling of well-being, but rather, that purposeful commitment to walk in obedience to the will of God as revealed to us through His Word.

I vividly recall in 1972, while serving the Lord in Papua, New Guinea, asking a group of Australian Bible school students who were visiting our work this question: "What area of the Tabernacle of Moses represents full spiritual maturity? The Outer Court, the Holy Place, or the Holy of Holies?" Almost immediately, everyone replied "The Holy of Holies." They were shocked when I informed them that they were all wrong. I then proceeded to tell them that true spiritual maturity is to know where to be in any given area at any given time. Jesus knew when to draw aside and spend time alone in prayer. He also knew when to be in the market place, healing the sick and casting out devils.

I think sometimes we tend to fall for the belief that spending hours and hours alone in worship and prayer constitutes true "intimacy." Doing some type of "outer court" routine is less spiritual. The secret to true friendship with God is being led by the Spirit. If the Spirit of God says "Come away, My beloved," then respond accordingly. If He says, "I must work the works of Him that sent Me," then roll up your sleeves and pitch in.

There is a danger in some circles of raising up a new generation of "monks and nuns," cloistered away in prayer centers around the country, enjoying the atmosphere created by sentimental music about bridal love while forgetting that the Bridegroom's passion is that "none should perish." Just as Jesus stated to the Pharisees, *"You are mistaken, not understanding the Scriptures nor the power of God"* so likewise we can be mistaken by worshiping and not working or working and not worshiping (see Matt. 22:29 NASB). Friendship with God involves both the Holy of Holies as well as ministering in the Outer Court.

COMMITMENT

There are times in any relationship where our feelings for each other may be tested. During these times it is our commitment to each other that triumphs over our feelings. I love the story of Ruth the young Moabitess, who after losing her husband was faced with a choice to either stay in the familiar surroundings of her home and country or move with Naomi to Bethlehem. Naomi urges her to stay, telling her she has nothing to offer as an incentive to go with her. Ruth, however, is committed to go, regardless of the cost. Her commitment is legendary and has been used repeatedly down through the years to inspire countless couples to true commitment as they take their marriage vows. Let's remind ourselves of her words:

> *But Ruth said, "Do not urge me to leave you or turn back from following you; for where you go, I will go, and where you lodge, I will lodge. Your people shall be my people, and your God, my God. Where you die, I will die, and there will I be buried. Thus may the Lord do to me, and worse, if anything but death parts you and me"* (Ruth 1:16-17 NASB).

Ruth's commitment reminds me of those in Revelation who *"follow the Lamb wherever He goes"* (Rev. 14:4 NASB). All of us would have loved to have followed the Lamb to the Mount of Transfiguration, there to gaze upon His eternal majesty and splendor and listen as He spoke to Moses and Elijah. However, it is another thing entirely to enter with Him into the Garden of Gethsemane and identify with Him in all of His pain and suffering, let alone follow Him to Calvary to be crucified. This is what it means to be truly committed. We resolve to "follow the Lamb" regardless of the circumstances or costs involved. Friendship involves commitment. We place our hands on the plough and refuse to look back. To Daniel, commitment meant the lion's den. To Joseph it meant rejection and false accusation. To Jeremiah it meant the pit. To Paul, it meant stoning and imprisonment. To John the Baptist, it meant getting beheaded. To John the beloved, it meant banishment. None of these godly saints would have described their ordeal as some emotional high, but rather that of being worthy to suffer for His Name. Proverbs declares, *"A friend loves at all times..."* (Prov. 17:17 NASB). This includes adversity as well as times of ecstasy.

May God grant you the grace to be His friend. There is no higher privilege.

ENDNOTE

1. Charles F. Stanley, *A Touch of His Freedom* (Grand Rapids, MI: Zondervan, 1991).

About Frank DeCenso, Jr.

Frank is the author of *Presence Powered Living: Building a Life of Intimacy and Partnership with God*, published by Vineyard International Publishers. His Web site is http://presencepowered.com. He lives in Virginia Beach, Virginia, with his wife of 15 years.

Other Books by Frank DeCenso, Jr.

Presence Powered Living: Building a Life of Intimacy and Partnership with God

More Information About the Authors

Che Ahn
www.harvestim.org

Sam Hinn
www. tgpworship.com

Christy Wimber
yorbalindavineyard.com

SJ Hill
www.sjhillonline.com

Ed Piorek
www.fatherlovesyou.com

Dr. Stephan Vosloo
www.crosscontact.org

Gary Wiens
www.burningheartmimistries.com

Marc A. Dupont
www.marcdupontministries.org

Dr. Peter Fitch
www.ssu.ca
www.scvine.com

Steve Long
www.tacf.org

David Ravenhill
www.davidravenhill.net

DESTINY IMAGE PUBLISHERS, INC.

*"Speaking to the Purposes of God for This Generation
and for the Generations to Come."*

Visit our new site home at
www.DestinyImage.com

Free Subscription to DI Newsletter

Receive free unpublished articles by top DI authors, exclusive

discounts, and free downloads from our best and newest books.

Visit www.destinyimage.com to subscribe.

Write to: Destiny Image

P.O. Box 310

Shippensburg, PA 17257-0310

Call: 1-800-722-6774

Email: orders@destinyimage.com

For a complete list of our titles or to place an order
online, visit www.destinyimage.com.

Find us on FACEBOOK or follow us on TWITTER.

www.facebook.com/destinyimage   facebook

www.twitter.com/destinyimage   twitter